A DEVOTIONAL SERIES for EXCEPTIONAL INDIVIDUALS and THEIR FAMILIES

CHAMPIONS CURRICULUM

Home Edition

By Sandra Robinson, Ph.D. and Pastor Craig Johnson
Illustrations by Mary Hancock

Why is family devotional time important?

There are over 30 million school aged students in America with special needs. Yet, less than one percent of churches in America have services or supports for these families. Hence, millions of families are unable to take their children and young adults to church because they are without adequate programs and services. This devotional is written for those families who aren't able to attend worship services. It is also written for those families who attend services and desire a family devotional time where all family members are able to participate. According to scripture, the greatest members of the kingdom of God are children.

> *At that time the disciples came to Jesus, saying, "Who then is greatest in the kingdom of heaven?" Then Jesus called a little child to Him, set him in the midst of them, and said, "Assuredly, I say to you, unless you are converted and become as little children you will by no means enter the kingdom of heaven"* (Matthew 18: 1-3).

Children are given a place of great honor by God. God has established that the greatest in His kingdom be members of a family. The family is the most important unit in society. God intended that we would be part of His heavenly family. The scripture says, *"God already planned to have us as His own children. This was done by Jesus Christ in His plan, God wanted this done"* (Ephesians 1:5, New Life Version). It is the family, both nuclear and extended, He entrusts to educate and nurture children. Families with children with special needs have been chosen by God to minister to these amazing individuals. Children and young adults learn by listening to and imitating their parents and other important people in their lives. If we want exceptional students to live a life committed to Christ, the adults in their lives must show them how to do it. God commands the family to teach each other how to have a relationship with God in a manner in which He desires.

> *Hear, O Israel: The Lord our God, the Lord is one. Love the Lord your God with all your heart and with all your soul and with all your strength. These commandments that I give you today are to be on your hearts. Impress them on your children. Talk about them when you sit at home and when you walk along the road, when you lie down and when you get up. Tie them as symbols on your hands and bind them on your foreheads. Write them on the door frames of your houses and on your gates* (Deuteronomy 6:5-9).

The Foundational Beliefs of these Devotionals

The devotionals in this book were created based on the following beliefs:

- All students, regardless of their abilities, are gifts from God and are made in His image reflecting His dignity.

- Exceptional students are not in need of treatment, but are vital members of society born to make a difference in this world through their relationship with God and others.

- At the core of every devotional is the understanding that believers in Christ are required to do two things on this earth. First, they are to love the Lord with all their heart, soul, mind, and strength. Secondly, they are asked to share His love with others.

- We believe that, regardless of the students' challenges, they are able to learn spiritual concepts and share what they have learned with others.

- The church is not asked to discern how God ministers to our students with special needs, but is charged to acknowledge that He does so in profound ways.

- We call our exceptional individuals Champions because they overcome many obstacles each day.

- Our actions, good or bad, begin with our thoughts. What we think often dictates how we feel, and how we feel influences how we act.

The Goal of these Devotionals

The goal of these devotionals is anchored in the definition of the word "devotion." The word "devotion" is defined as a love, loyalty, or enthusiasm for a person, activity, or cause (Oxford Dictionary, 2014). We show our devotion to God by worshiping Him through music, praying, and studying His Word. The goal of these easy-to-read Biblically based activities is to increase the Champions' and their family members' love for and knowledge of God. They also provide practical ways to share His love with others.

The first step in being devoted to others is to learn how to make and maintain friendships. Social emotional skills are the foundation for beginning, developing, and maintaining relationships. Social emotional skills include the students' ability to: identify and manage personal emotions, accurately identify the emotional states of others, understand and show empathy, make and sustain eye contact, understand different perspectives, take turns, share, ask for help, offer help, problem solve, handle challenging social situations constructively, and establish and maintain positive relationships with God others (Zins, Weissbert, Wang, & Walberg, 2004; Robinson & Johnson, 2012).

Many exceptional students have difficulty developing social emotional skills, but with instruction they can improve those skills. These devotionals teach students that our feelings are a special system designed by God. They provide us with information about the world around us. What we think dictates how we feel, and how we feel influences our actions. Consequently, if we control our thoughts, we can control our actions. If we want to change our actions, we must change our thoughts.

Our Thoughts $\longrightarrow$ Our Feelings $\longrightarrow$ Our Actions

To assist with this process, these devotionals include feeling faces. Each face reflects a particular emotion or feeling explored in the devotionals. There are six faces and each face is found at the beginning of each set of devotionals that focuses on that particular feeling.

The Benefits of Family Devotionals

There are many benefits of having family devotionals:

- They promote family unity and love by providing time for families to communicate and demonstrate their love for each other. *"Love one another as I have loved you"* (John 13:34).

- It fulfills the God-given responsibility of parents to their children. The Word of God requires parents to provide for their children. The provision is not solely material things, but spiritual nurturing and guidance. The Bible says if we don't provide for our families, we are no better than those who are not believers. *"But if anyone does not provide for his relatives, and especially for members of his household, he has denied the faith and is worse than an unbeliever"*(1 Timothy 5:8, English Standard Version). We define a believer as someone who believes that Jesus is Lord and that God raised him from the dead (Romans 10:9). Believers ask Jesus to be their Savior and have a personal relationship with him.

- It secures our children's future. God promises parents that if they teach their children His ways, their children will not forget them and one day will embrace them as their own. Part of training a child in the ways of the Lord is modeling the behaviors that please God. Modeling the appropriate behaviors is often not enough for exceptional students to demonstrate them. These behaviors must also be discussed and practiced. Family devotionals provide a good time to facilitate the acquisition of behaviors that please God. *"Train up a child in the way he should go, and when he is old he will not depart from it."* (Proverbs 22:6).

    Children, obey your parents in the Lord for this is right. Honor your father and mother (this is the first commandment with a promise), *that it may go well with you and that you may live long in the land. Fathers, do not provoke your children to anger, but bring them up in the discipline and instruction of the Lord* (Ephesians 6: 1-4, English Standard Version).

- Having a family devotional time promotes communication among family members which in turn reduces conflict. These devotionals teach us how to manage our feelings. They teach us positive ways to handle difficult situations. *"Everyone should be quick to listen, slow to speak, and slow to become angry"* (James 1:19).

- It prepares the family for difficult times. The Bible stories in this devotional book teach exceptional students and their family members to trust God in difficult times.

    Jesus said, "Everyone who hears these words of mine and puts them into practice is like a wise man who built his house on the rock. The rain came down, the streams rose, and the winds blew and beat against that house; yet it did not fall, because it had its foundation on the rock" (Matthew 7:24-25).

Devotional Development

These devotionals are adapted from the Champions Curriculum. The curriculum was developed using the Universal Design for Learning (UDL). UDL is a set of principles for designing a curriculum that provides equal access for all exceptional students. When UDL is used to develop curriculum, the concepts taught can be understood by individuals with challenges in their abilities to comprehend, see, hear, speak, move, read, write, attend, organize, think, and remember. The curriculum, and consequently these devotionals, were developed using the following guidelines:

- Each devotional has one key concept.

- Exceptional students differ in the ways in which they perceive and comprehend the information presented to them. Therefore, a multi-sensory instructional approach is essential to the teaching and learning process. These devotionals were written to engage individuals' senses which will increase their understanding and retention of the concepts taught.

- The appropriate accommodations and modifications have been incorporated into each devotional to ensure learning.

- The materials are attractive and engaging.

These devotions are for all ages and family groups. Everyone can benefit from studying God's Word and applying its principles to daily life. Each devotional includes the following elements:

Scripture - Each devotional has a scripture that corresponds with the Bible story.

Materials - These devotionals can be implemented with common objects found around the house. For every devotional, you will need writing utensils and a Bible.

Goal - Each devotional has a goal. Goals are important because they give the family a clear focus for their time together and provide a feeling of accomplishment at the conclusion of the devotional. The goal is presented in two formats. The first is simple sentences. The second is an equation with conceptual chunks. The equation format takes one concept and adds another to formulate the overall goal of the devotional.

Object lesson - The object lesson is a concrete illustration of an abstract concept. The family members' attention is captured by the use of household objects to convey the lesson's objective.

Vocabulary - The vocabulary segment of the devotional assists family members in understanding the key concepts being taught. Vocabulary development is critical to academic success because it improves comprehension and communication.

Application -This segment of the lesson focuses on the integration of newly learned concepts into real life situations.

Declarations - The declarations were written by Pastor Craig Johnson. Declarations are statements of faith we speak over our lives and the lives of others. There are two declarative statements. One is for the family and the other is specifically written for the Champion.

Prayer - Each lesson includes a prayer the family is encouraged to pray. It serves as a model for prayer. Some individuals are uncomfortable praying out loud. Prayer is having a conversation with God. There are four elements to each prayer in the devotional:

- Hi God

- Thank God

- Help me God

- Thank God

We can remember these four elements by their initials; HTHT. "Thank God" is two of the four aspects of the prayer. The Bible is very clear on what our attitude should be in all situations. I Thessalonians 5:18 says, "Give thanks in all circumstances; for this is God's will for you in Christ Jesus."

How to Use This Book

There are 31 family devotionals in this book. There is one for each day of the month. Repetition is key for exceptional individuals to learn and retain concepts; therefore, frequent revisiting the concepts taught in these devotionals is encouraged. The devotionals are organized by emotion which include; happiness, sadness, fear, anxiety, and anger. The devotionals in each unit assist family members in identifying and regulating the emotion explored in the unit.

Set aside time to complete the devotionals daily. Memorize the scripture in each devotional. Do this by posting the verse where it can be easily seen. Read the scripture out loud often during the day. Look for ways to apply what was discussed during devotional time to real life situations.

We believe that as you read God's Word and put the spiritual concepts into practice, God will bless you and use you to bless others.

Choose to be happy.

Robinson and Johnson

Devotional 1
Choose to Be Happy

Materials needed - 2 lemons (1 with peel and 1 without), 1 pitcher filled with water, the happy face

Scripture - Philippians 4:4 - *Rejoice in the Lord always. I will say again: Rejoice!*

Goal - We will understand how to stay happy no matter what is happening in our lives.

I feel unhappy. + I think about God's Word and praise Him. = I am happy.

Object lesson - Before the devotional begins, set aside a pitcher filled with water, and one lemon with the peel and one without. Show your family members the peeled lemon and say, "Life is like this lemon. Sometimes life is sour and bitter. It doesn't taste good because there are a lot of things that happen that cause us to be anxious, sad, or afraid." Discuss some of these situations with your family. For example someone I love is sick, I am lonely, or my pet ran away. Drop the peeled lemon in the pitcher and watch it sink. Say, "Sometimes it feels like we are sinking and have no control over the negative things happening in our lives." Remove the lemon without the peel and place the lemon with the peel in the pitcher. Tell your family, "The lemon doesn't sink because the peel keeps the water out of the lemon. Water adds weight to the fruit and causes it to sink. God gives us protection against feelings of anxiety, sadness, and fear. That protection is His Word, the Bible. The protection is like the peel of the lemon. When we read His Word and do what it says, we can float above all the negative feelings just like the lemon floats on top of the water. We can be happy no matter what is happening in our lives." Show your family the happy face.

Vocabulary development - Introduce the vocabulary words to the family. Talk about the meaning of each word. Acting out the meaning of the words through mime and gestures increases the understanding of the concepts.

Happiness - a good feeling about something
Thoughts - your ideas
Feelings - your emotions
Actions - what you do
Rejoice - celebrate, cheer, be glad

Bible lesson – Look at the scripture card and point out the features of the picture while you read the Bible story out loud. Read the scripture out loud and have your family members repeat it several times. After you read the Bible story, discuss the following questions with your family. Color the scripture card together.

- What were Paul and Silas doing before they were put in jail?
- What did they do when they were in jail?
- What happened when they began praising God?
- What did the jailer do as a result of what God did for Paul and Silas?

Application - Say: "What we think affects how we feel, and how we feel influences how we act." Discuss the diagram with the family.

Our Thoughts ⟶ Our Feelings ⟶ Our Actions

Say to your family, "Sometimes things happen in our lives that cause us to feel happy. Look at the happy face. Happiness is a good feeling about something. Sometimes it feels like; a warm feeling in my heart, a tickling feeling on my skin, and/or my muscles are relaxed. When people are happy they often smile and laugh."

Continue with, "When we feel unhappy, we can change our feelings to happiness by changing what we are thinking. God's Word states it is important to think about the positive things in our lives. It also says to rejoice and give thanks to God, no matter what we are going through. Praising God helps us become comfortable and happy. Here are some things to remember to praise God for:

- Thank Him for His love for you.
- Praise Him for being your Savior.
- Thank Him for His care and comfort.
- Praise Him for giving you a family and friends."

Review the scripture verse with your family.

Family Declaration: We declare we will choose to be happy in every situation. Even when something difficult happens we will take a breath, smile, and find something to be grateful for. We will choose to do the right thing even when we may not feel like it. Because of our obedience, God will make our day brighter and take us higher than we have ever been before. This is our declaration!

Champion: I declare I will choose to be happy. Even when something difficult happens I will find something to be grateful for. I will do the right thing even when I don't feel like it. Because I am obedient, God will make my day brighter and take me higher than ever before. This is my declaration!

Family Prayer – Read the family prayer together.

Dear God,

Thank You for being with us even when we are not happy. Help us think about You now and when we are not happy. Thank You for all the blessings You have given us, especially Your son Jesus. Thank You for your Word, the Bible, that teaches us how to live our lives. Amen.

Paul and Silas
Scripture Card

Philippians 4:4 - Rejoice in the Lord always. I will say it again: Rejoice!

Paul and Silas
Scripture Card

Paul and Silas were leaders in the early church. They loved God and people, so everywhere they went they told people about God's love and salvation through Jesus Christ. While visiting Greece, they were beaten and put in jail for helping a young woman.

Paul and Silas didn't do anything wrong, yet they were in a dark, cold, bad place. They had no reason to be happy, but they knew that no matter where they were, God was with them. They began to pray and sing praises to God.

The other prisoners were listening to them. Suddenly, there was a violent earthquake and the prison doors flew open. All the chains of the prisoners came loose. The jailer saw this happen and knew it was a miracle. He was frightened that Paul and Silas would leave and he would be punished for their escape. They didn't leave, but shared the story of Jesus with him, and the jailer accepted Jesus as his Savior. He invited Paul and Silas to his home for dinner that night.

It was a miracle. The jailer who saw the whole thing asked Jesus into his heart and invited Paul and Silas to his home for dinner.

Even when bad things happen to us, we can still be happy because God is with us and He can turn our bad situation into something we can be happy about. Adapted from Acts 16:11-40.

Philippians 4:4 - Rejoice in the Lord always. I will say it again: Rejoice!

Devotional 2

Sharing with Others Pleases God

Materials needed - a special snack or hand-held video game/toy/iPod/iPad and the happy face

Scripture - **Hebrews 13:16** - *Share with others because it makes God happy (adapted).*

Goal - We will understand that sharing pleases God and makes us happy.

I have something to share. + I share it with others. = God is pleased and I am happy.

Object lesson - While you are seated, have one family member eat a special snack or play with a special video game. Have them look like they are really enjoying it. Tell the individual not to share his\her object with anyone. Ask the family members who didn't have the opportunity to play with the object or eat the snack, "How did you feel when you saw that only one family member was able to enjoy eating the snack or playing with the object? God has given us so many wonderful gifts. It pleases Him when we share with others. We also feel good when we share." Show your family the happy face.

Vocabulary development - Introduce the vocabulary words to the family. Talk about the meaning of each word. Acting out the meaning of the words through mime and gestures increases the understanding of the concepts.

Share - giving part of what you have to others
Sacrifice - act of giving up something you want

Bible lesson – Look at the scripture card and point out the features of the picture while you read the Bible story out loud. Read the scripture out loud and have your family members repeat it several times. After you read the Bible story, discuss the following questions with your family. Color the scripture card together.

- What did Jesus teach others when He was on the earth?
- How many people came to hear Jesus?
- What did the people need?
- How did Jesus get them what they needed?

Application - Use the *Sharing Conversation Cards* as you model how to share with others. Help your family learn to share by reviewing the steps with them. Conversation cards may be used to increase an individual's social skills. The cards can be left in the devotional book or removed from the book. To make conversation cards, remove the page, cut out the cards, and punch a hole in the upper left hand corner of each card. Place the cards in sequential order on a small metal ring.

Review the scripture verse with your family often.

Family Declaration: We declare we will find something we can give away to someone every day. People need what we have to give. The greatest thing we can do is be good to someone else in the midst of our challenges. We will not let our circumstances stop us from sharing with others. We know when we build others, God will build us. This is our declaration!

Champion: I declare I will share what God has given me. God will honor me when I help others. People need what I have to give. The more I share, the happier I will be. I know when I build others, God will build me. This is my declaration!

Family Prayer – Read the family prayer together.

Dear God,

Thank You for giving us so many wonderful things to share. Help us learn how to share our things with others. Thank You for sharing Your Son Jesus with all of us. Amen.

The Boy Who Shared his Lunch
Scripture Card

Hebrews 13:16 - Share with others because it makes God happy (adapted).

The Boy Who Shared his Lunch
Scripture Card

When Jesus was with us on the earth, he spent a lot of time teaching people how to love and obey God and how to treat others. Many people came to hear Him teach. On one particular day, about 5,000 people came to listen to Jesus. At the end of the day, the people were hungry and there was no food to fed them. Two disciples, who were close friends of Jesus, suggested that Jesus send away the people so they could go find a place to buy food. A boy, standing near by, heard this and offered to share his lunch with Jesus and the others. The boy had five loaves of bread and two fish. Jesus smiled at the boy and said, "Thank you for sharing."

Jesus told the people to sit down. He thanked God in heaven for the food and told the disciples to pass the food out to all the people. Everyone had enough to eat and there was a lot of food left over. The boy who shared his lunch was amazed by all the left over food. He asked Jesus, "How did this happen? Everyone got something to eat and there was a lot of food left over." Jesus replied, "When you share with others, God makes sure there is enough for everyone." The boy was so happy that he had shared his lunch. Adapted from Matthew 14: 13-21.

Hebrews 13:16 - Share with others because it makes God happy (adapted).

Sharing with Others Pleases God   Devotional 2

Sharing Conversation Cards

Use the Sharing Conversation Cards as you model how to share with others. Review the steps often to improve sharing skills.

1 Say, "Would you like to share my snack?"

Wait for your friend to answer.

2 If your friend says, "Yes," then share.

3 If your friend says, "No," say,

"Ok, maybe next time."

please

thank you

Devotional 3

Jesus Receives a Compliment from His Father

Materials needed - the happy face

Scripture - I Thessalonians 5:11 - *Continue to encourage each other (adapted).*

Goal - We will understand the importance of encouraging each other through compliments.

I say something nice to my friend. + My friend is happy. = God is pleased, and I am happy.

Object lesson - Encourage the family members to look at the Compliment Tree, and then tell them the following, "This is a Compliment Tree. It is a special kind of tree. There are leaves on the tree, but nothing is written on them. They are not alive unless they have a compliment written on them. It is the leaves on a tree that help make it grow. The leaves take in sunlight and other things and make food for the plant so it can grow. Compliments can help people grow"

Continue with, "A compliment is saying something nice to others about how they act or what they look like. Think about your family members and write a compliment about each family member on each leaf. Let's read the compliments out loud." Remind your family that it is the leaves on the tree that help it grow and when we compliment others that encourages them to grow. It makes them happy and us happy.

It is important that respectful language such as, "Thank you," "Please," and "Excuse me" be used during the exchange of compliments.

Vocabulary development - Introduce the vocabulary words to the family. Talk about the meaning of each word. Acting out the meaning of the words through mime and gestures increases the understanding of the concepts.

> **Continue** - to not stop; to keep doing something, to keep going
> **Compliment** - saying something nice to someone about how they act, or what they look like

Bible lesson – Look at the scripture card and point out the features of the picture while you read the Bible story out loud. Read the scripture out loud and have your family members repeat it several times. After you read the Bible story, discuss the following questions with your family. Color the scripture card together.

- What did John the Baptist do as he went from town-to-town?
- What was unusual about John the Baptist?
- Why is it important to get baptized?
- Jesus received a compliment from His Father. What did His Father say about Him?

Application - We can also compliment others without using our voices. This is called non-verbal communication. The actions are called gestures. Gestures are visible bodily actions which communicate a message.

Practice giving each other non-verbal compliments such as a thumbs-up, high-five, a smile, fist pound, touch your eyes and smile for a compliment regarding the eyes, and touch your hair and smile for a compliment regarding the hair. Give others a compliment (either verbal or non verbal) often.

Review the scripture verse with your family often.

Family Declaration: We declare we are encouragers. When we encourage others, we will be encouraged. We will look for the best in people as God brings out the best in us. We will speak life over others and ourselves. We are more than conquerors. We are the head and not the tail. We are above and not beneath. We can do all things through Christ who strengthens us. This is our declaration!

Champion: I declare I am an encourager. As I encourage others I will be encouraged. I will look for the best in people. I will speak life over others and myself. I am more than a conqueror. I am the head and not the tail. I am above and not beneath. I can do all things through Christ who strengthens me. This is my declaration!

Family Prayer – Read the family prayer together.

Hi God,

Thank You for the greatest compliment. You think we are so valuable that You sent Your Son Jesus to earth to show us how to live our lives. We want to make You happy by complimenting others. Help us compliment others so they feel happy. Thank You for making us happy. Amen.

Our Family
Compliment
Tree

Think about your family members and write a compliment on each leaf. Read the compliments out loud.

Jesus Receives a Compliment from His Father

Scripture Card

"This is my Son, whom I love;
with Him I am well pleased"
(Matthew 3: 17).

I Thessalonians 5:11 - Continue to encourage each other (adapted).

Jesus Receives a Compliment from His Father
Scripture Card

In Jesus' time, there was a man named John the Baptist. He went from town-to-town telling people they needed to ask God to forgive them of their sins and be baptized. Being baptized is like taking a bath with your clothes on. Being baptized is a way to let everyone know that you have asked God for forgiveness and want to live a life doing what God tells you to do.

John was an interesting person. He didn't care about having a home, certain food, or particular clothes. He lived in the desert. He wore an outfit of camel's hair and a leather belt. He ate insects like locusts (which look like grasshoppers) and wild honey. All he cared about was telling others about God.

When people heard that John was in the area, they would come from all over to listen to him and to get baptized. Some thought John the Baptist was the Savior. He told them that He was baptizing them now, but very soon the Savior of the world was coming.

John continued to preach and baptize people, until one day Jesus came by to be baptized. John told Jesus that he couldn't baptize Him because John was just an ordinary man and Jesus was the Savior. Jesus insisted that John baptize Him because it was the right thing to do, so John baptized Jesus. As soon as Jesus was baptized, a dove came out of the sky and landed on Jesus' shoulder and a voice from heaven said, "This is my Son. I love Him and I am pleased with Him." Jesus' heavenly Father gave Him a compliment. Jesus was happy that He had pleased His Father. Adapted from Matthew 3:13-17.

I Thessalonians 5:11 - Continue to encourage each other (adapted).

Devotional 4

I Can Use My Gifts to Make Others Happy

Materials needed - slips of paper, marker, gift bag, a few inexpensive school supplies, wrapped candies, and the happy face.

Scripture - Romans 12:6 - *We have different gifts, according to the grace given to each of us (adapted).*

Goal - We all have special abilities, or gifts, given to us by God. God has given us these gifts to help others.

I have a gift(s). + I use my gift(s) to make others happy. = God is pleased and I am happy.

Object lesson - Have a slip of paper with the name of each family member written on it. Fold it in half and place it in a gift bag. Have each family member choose a slip of paper, pull it out of the bag, and read the name on the paper without telling anyone. Have a variety of small inexpensive gifts on a cookie sheet. Some examples of inexpensive gifts would be school supplies, stickers, or individually wrapped candies. Have each family member think about the person they selected and choose a gift they think the person would like. Answer the following questions in your mind. What does he/she like? What are his/her hobbies or things the person likes doing? Have each family member select a gift for the individual whose name they choose, and give the gift to him/her.

thank you

Tell your family, "We are all gifted. We all have special abilities given to us by God. They are not gifts that we can touch. They are gifts like being a good teacher, builder, helper, singer, or artist. God has given us these gifts to help others. When we help others, it makes us feel happy and it pleases God." Show your family the happy face. Continue with, "God gives the best gifts. He is a fantastic gift giver. He gave us a Savior, Jesus."

Vocabulary development - Introduce the vocabulary words to the family. Talk about the meaning of each word. Acting out the meaning of the words through mime and gestures increases the understanding of the concepts.

Gift - something given to you by God that you didn't have to pay for
Grace - God's generous and unexpected gift of love and mercy freely given to us

Bible lesson - Look at the scripture card and point out the features of the picture while you read the Bible story out loud. Read the scripture out loud and have your family members repeat it several times. After you read the Bible story, discuss the following questions with your family. Color the scripture card together.

- Why did the master give the servants coins?
- What did the master do to the servant with one (1) gold coin? Why?
- What did the master do to the servant with two (2) gold coins? Why?
- What did the master do to the servant with five (5) gold coins? Why?
- What should we do with our gifts and talents?

Application - Say, "God has given each of us a gift. Your gift is your talent or ability. In other words, it is something you do well or like to do. God wants us to use the gifts we have to make others happy. This pleases God. God's word says in **Romans 12:6** -*We have different gifts, according to the grace given to each of us.*

Discuss the gifts on the *Using My Gifts to Make Others Happy* document. Read and discuss the activities under each gifting. Now have your family members select individuals they would like to make happy and write the names of the individuals next to the activities. Show your family the happy face.

Review the scripture verse with your family often. Encourage your family members to fulfill their commitment.

Family Declaration: We declare we are gifted and talented. We are uniquely created to make a difference in people. God has a special plan for our lives. As we trust Him, God will reveal His purpose. We will never hold back our special ability to bring hope to others. We don't have to help people, we get to help people. Our greatest purpose is about to unfold. This is our declaration!

Champion: I declare I am gifted and talented. God created me to do great things. He has a special plan for my life. I have unique abilities that can touch others like no one else can. I don't have to help people, I get to help people. My greatest purpose is about to unfold. This is my declaration!

Family Prayer – Read the family prayer together.

Dear God,

Thank You for giving us spiritual gifts. Help us know how and when to use them. Thank You for giving us the greatest gift of all-Jesus. Please help us remember to use our gifts to make others happy because this makes You happy. Amen.

Using My Gifts Pleases God
Scripture Card

Romans 12:6 - We have different gifts, according to the grace given to each of us...
(adapted).

Using My Gifts Pleases God
Scripture Card

Jesus told the disciples a story about using the gifts and talents God gave them to help others. In this story, the master of a house went on a long journey. He gave gold coins to his servants and asked them to use the gold coins to help others. To one servant, he gave five bags of gold coins, to another he have two bags of gold coins, and to the third servant he gave one bag of gold coins.

When the master of the house returned from his journey, he asked all the servants to come and tell him what they did with the gold coins. The man who received five bags of coins and the servant who received two bags, used their coins to do good things. The man with five bags of coins now had ten bags. The servant with two bags now had four bags. When these two servants came to the master and showed him what they had done, the master was very happy. He told them, "Good job!"

The servant who was given one bag of gold coins came to the master and showed him that he still had just one bag of gold coins. He had buried his coins and had not used them to do any good. The master said, "You didn't do good things with the gold coins, so I am going to take away your bag and give it to the servant who has ten bags of coins."

Jesus wants us to use our gifts, talents, and abilities to help others. This makes God, others, and ourselves happy. Adapted from Matthew 25:14-30.

Romans 12:6 - We have different gifts, according to the grace given to each of us... (adapted).

I Can Use My Gifts to Make Others Happy   Devotional 4

Using My Gifts to Make Others Happy

Read and discuss the activities under each gifting with your family. Have each family member select someone he/she would like to make happy. Have the family members write the names of the people next to the activity they selected to do for them. Encourage your family members to fulfill their commitment.

Teacher	Helper	Builder	Music	Art
I can teach someone how to do something.	When others are sick, I can get them something they need.	I can help my friend build something.	I can play a song for someone to make them feel better.	I can make a card for others to help them feel better.
I can read a story or tell a story to someone.	I can help others by opening the door for them, or helping them clean up, like washing the dishes.	When something is broken, I can help fix it.	I can sing a song for someone to make them feel better.	I can make a craft for someone to make them feel happy.

I Can Use My Gifts to Make Others Happy   Devotional 4

Using My Gifts to Make Others Happy

Read and discuss the activities under each gifting with your family. Have each family member select someone he/she would like to make happy. Have each family member write the name of the person next to the activity he/she selected to do for that individual. Encourage your family members during the week to fulfill their commitment.

Technology	Physical	Leadership	Spiritual	Nature
I can teach someone how to use a new computer game or application.	I can help my family by...	I can encourage others to do something new.	I can tell others about how much Jesus loves them.	I can take care of my pets by feeding them, walking them, and cleaning up after them.
I can help someone play a video game or do a puzzle.	I can help others with yard work or taking out their trash.	I can invite others to church.	I can pray for others.	I can help keep nature beautiful by picking up trash when I see it outdoors.

Devotional 5

Friendships Bring Happiness

Materials needed - a hand-sized ball of yarn, a hand-sized rubber ball, and the happy face

Scripture - Ecclesiastes 4: 9, 10 - *Two people are better than one because they can help each other (adapted).*

Goal - We will understand that Jesus is our best friend and He wants us to be friends with others.

Jesus is my best friend. + He can help me make new friends. = I am happy.

Object lesson - Tell your family, "Friends are people who care about you and want to help you. Friends act a certain way and that's how we know they are our friends. Family members can also be friends. Let's talk about the qualities we have that make us good friends." Hold onto a ball of yarn by the string end and firmly toss the ball to someone in your family as you say out loud why you think he/she is a good friend. Encourage everyone to take a turn doing this. Encourage your family members to hold onto the string tightly. When everyone has had a turn, say: "Look at the yarn and notice that everyone is connected. We are all here doing something together. For many of us, Jesus is our best friend. Jesus also wants us to make new friends. We make and keep friends through being together and having conversations. Having Jesus as our best friend and making friends with others brings happiness." Show your family the happy face.

Vocabulary development - Introduce the vocabulary words to the family. Talk about the meaning of each word. Acting out the meaning of the words through mime and gestures often increase the understanding of the concepts.

    Conversation - the spoken exchange of thoughts, opinions, and feelings; talking
    Difficult - hard to do, requires a lot of planning and effort
    Jealous - feeling of being angry at someone because they have what you want

Bible Lesson - Look at the scripture card and point out the features of the picture while you read the Bible story out loud. Read the scripture out loud and have your family members repeat it several times. After you read the Bible story, discuss the following questions with your family. Color the scripture card together.

- What was David's job at King Saul's palace?
- Who was David's good friend?
- What qualities did Jonathan have that made him a good friend to David?
- How did Jonathan protect David?
- What did David become when he got older?

Application - Say, "What are the qualities of a good friend?" Identify and discuss the qualities of a good friend. Some examples would include being honest, loyal, a good listener, trusting, fun to be around, and caring. Jesus has all these qualities. He wants you to have these qualities. God created us to be best friends with Him, but He also wants us to have other friends and to be a friend to others.

Friendship begins with conversations. Having a conversation with someone is like playing a game of catch. When someone says something to you, he is throwing you an imaginary ball he wants you to catch. When you catch the ball, he is waiting for you to throw the conversation ball back to him. In order to throw the conversation ball back to him, you need to pay attention to what he says so you can make a comment that is on topic.

Conversations have three (3) steps. The steps to conversation are a greeting, sustaining a conversation, and ending a conversation. A greeting makes others feel good because you are paying attention to them. Some ways to greet others using your voice are, "Hi", "Hello", "How's it going?", or "What's up?". You can greet someone without saying a word by nodding your head, smiling, or waving. There are several ways to continue a conversation. We can ask questions about the topic, or give additional information on the topic, or tell our own story regarding the topic. It is important to stay on the topic of discussion. Changing the topic frequently is confusing and uncomfortable to others. You can end the conversation by saying, "Bye", "See you later", or "Have a good day".

Review the steps to having a conversation. Use the ***Having a Conversation Conversation Cards*** to practice having a conversation with your family members. The cards will serve as a visual and tactile prompt. You may use a conversation ball to assist students as they practice having a conversation. Give a medium size ball to the individual initiating the conversation. When they are done talking, they give their partner the ball. Only the individual with the ball is able to speak.

Steps to Having a Conversation

Step 1: Greeting. Say or wave, "Hi."

Step 2: Keep the conversation going by adding information about the topic, telling a story about the topic, or asking questions about the topic.

Step 3: Wait for others to respond to the comments.

Step 4: End the conversation by saying or waving, "Bye."

Family Declaration: We declare we are building stronger relationships with each other and our friends. There is no relationship more important than our relationship with God. When we put Him first in our lives, He will give us influence and favor with others. We will go out of our way to be kind to people. Amazing new friendships are about to bloom. This is our declaration!

Champion: I declare I am building new friendships. There is nothing more important than my relationship with God. He is my best friend. When I put Him first, He is happy and I am happy. I will be kind to others and make new friends. God has amazing friendships coming my way. This is my declaration!

Review the scripture verse with your family often.

Family Prayer – Read the family prayer together.

Dear God, Thank You Jesus for being our best friend. Please help us learn how to be a good friend to You. Help us show You how much we love You every day. Amen.

Jonathan and David's Friendship
Scripture Card

Ecclesiastes 4:9-10 - Two people are better than one because they can help each other (adapted).

Jonathan and David's Friendship
Scripture Card

David was a shepherd boy who grew up to be the king of Israel. Before he was king, he had an important job in King Saul's palace. When King Saul was upset, he called David to play worship music to calm him.

Saul had a son named Jonathan. Jonathan and David spent a lot of time together. They had a lot of conversations about things that interested them. They were best friends.

Throughout his life, David fought many battles to protect Israel. God blessed David, and whenever he went to battle for the people of God, he won. Soon the people of God began to like David better than the king. King Saul became very jealous of David.

Saul told his son Jonathan and all the people who served him in the palace to kill David. Jonathan reminded his father Saul of all the good things David had done for the kingdom. Saul listened to Jonathan and promised not to harm David.

Later that day, Jonathan told David about Saul's promise. Not long after that, Saul felt distressed and he sent for David to play music to calm him. When Saul saw David he became more and more angry. He grabbed his spear and threw it at David. David ran out of the palace and hid. Jonathan found him and told David to leave the city quickly before Saul found him and killed him.

Jonathan protected David from his father, King Saul. David lived a long life because Jonathan was his friend and protected him. Adapted from I Samuel 18-20.

Ecclesiastes 4:9-10 - Two people are better than one because they can help each other (adapted).

Friendships bring Happiness   Devotional 5

Having a Conversation Conversation Cards

Use the Conversation Cards as you model how to have conversations with others.

1 Greeting. Say or wave, "Hi."

2 Keep the conversation going by telling a story about something that happened.

3 Wait for others to respond to your story.

4 Ending the conversation by saying or waving, "OK Bye."

Devotional 6

The Greatest Gift

Materials needed - a gift wrapped box with a picture of Jesus in it, and the happy face.

Scripture - Mark 12:30 - *Love the Lord your God with all your heart, soul, mind, and strength (adapted).*

Goal - We will understand that Jesus is the greatest gift we have ever received. When we think about Him, we can be happy.

God gave us the greatest gift, Jesus. + I will give my life to God. = I am happy, and God is happy.

Object lesson - Say, "It's Christmastime and there are a lot of things that are great about Christmas." Tell your family that everyone enjoys receiving gifts. Ask your family members to share about a favorite gift they have received. Show your family the wrapped gift and tell them that the gift is from God. Have them guess what is in the box. Have every one take turns unwrapping a portion of the gift. Open the box and show everyone the picture of Jesus.

Say, "Jesus is the greatest gift God has ever or will ever give us. Jesus came to teach us the right way to live. He taught us that loving and helping others will make us happy. He gave His life for us. If we believe that He is God's son and ask God to forgive our sins, we can live with God forever. This brings us so much happiness." Show your family the happy face.

Vocabulary development - Introduce the vocabulary words to the family. Talk about the meaning of each word. Acting out the meaning of the words through mime and gestures increases the understanding of the concepts. After you read the Bible story, discuss the following questions with your family.

Heart - the emotional/feeling part of a person
Soul - the spiritual part of a person
Mind - the thinking part of a person
Strength - the physical part of a person

Bible Lesson - Look at the scripture card and point out the features of the picture while you read the Bible story out loud. Read the scripture out loud and and have your family members repeat it several times. After you read the Bible story, discuss the following questions with your family. Color the scripture card together.

1. Who were Jesus' earthly parents?
2. Where was Jesus born?
3. How do you celebrate Jesus' birth?
4. Why is Jesus the greatest gift you have ever been given?
5. What is the greatest gift we can give God?

Application - Look at the document entitled, *My Gift to God is Me*. Look at the outline of the body. Point to the part of the body as you read the following, "God wants us to love Him with all of our minds. Our thoughts are in our mind. The first step in loving God is to think about what God is like, and what He likes.

- Think about how God made us because He wanted us in the world. He made us to be with Him. **Jeremiah 1:5** - *Before I formed you in the womb I knew you, before you were born I set you apart; I appointed you as a prophet to the nations.*

- Think about how His love for us never ends. **Jeremiah 31:3** - *I have loved you with an everlasting love; I have drawn you with loving-kindness.*

- Think about the fact that we make God happy. He has written a love song about us, and for us. **Zephaniah 3:17** - *The Lord your God is with you. He is strong and He will save you. He sings songs about you (adapted).*

- Think about how God gave us the greatest gift, Jesus. If we were the only one in the world who needed a Savior, Jesus still would have died on the cross for us. **John 3:16** - *For God so loved the world, that he gave His only son, that whoever believes in Him should not perish but have eternal life.*

Draw a picture or write words around the head of the figure to remind you of what God is like.

Say, "God wants us to love Him with all our heart. From our thoughts come our feelings. Our feelings are in our heart. When we think about all the reasons God is lovable, it is easy to love Him with all our feelings. Color the heart red. God wants us to love Him with all our soul. Our soul is our spirit. Since God is a spirit, He made us with a spirit so we could have a relationship with Him. The spirit is not visible. It is the part of us that lives forever. Color the soul blue. Often from our feelings come our actions. God wants us to love Him with all our strength. Loving God with all our strength means we express our love for Him through our actions. Our actions show how much we love Him.

Our thoughts (Mind) ➡ Our feelings (Heart) ➡ Our actions (Strength)

Discuss ways to show God how much we love Him. Here are some suggestions:

- Sing Him a love song.
- Write Him a love letter.
- Draw Him a picture.
- Help someone else.

- Obey your parents.
- Compliment others.
- Share your things with others.

Draw a picture or write words to represent how you will show God how much you love Him. Encourage your family members to perform at least one of the actions discussed each day. Review the scripture verse with your family often.

Family Declaration: We declare that God is good and He is meeting every need in our lives. When we love God and give him our very best, He will go before us making crooked paths straight. We know any difficulty we face is not permanent. We will overcome our challenges because greater is He who is in us than he that is in the world. We are God's most prized possession and He is our greatest gift. This is our declaration!

Champion: I declare that God is good and He is meeting all of my needs. When I give my life to God, He will fight for me in every situation. I will overcome my challenges because God is bigger than anything I will face. I am God's most prized possession and He is my greatest gift. This is my declaration!

Family Prayer – Read the family prayer together.

Dear God, Thank You for giving us the greatest gift we have ever received, Jesus. Help us to show You how much we love You every day. Thank You for allowing us to be with You always. Amen.

Jesus is the greatest gift.

The Greatest Gift
Scripture Card

Mark 12:30 - Love the Lord your God with all your heart, soul, mind, and strength (adapted).

The Greatest Gift
Scripture Card

Mary, a virgin, was living in Galilee. She was engaged to be married to Joseph, a Jewish carpenter. An angel visited her and explained to her that she would have a son and she would call him Jesus. Mary became pregnant by the Holy Spirit with Jesus. Joseph knew Mary was pregnant with the Savior of the world so he married her to take care of her. In those days, everyone had to go to the place where they were born to be counted. So Joseph took Mary to Bethlehem. While they were there, the time came for Jesus to be born. The town was full of people. There were no rooms at the local inns for them to stay, so they stayed in a stable with the animals.

In the nearby field, there were shepherds watching their sheep. An angel of the Lord appeared to them and they were terrified. The angel said to them, "Do not be afraid. I bring you good news that will cause great joy for all the people. Today, in the town of Bethlehem the Savior of the World has been born. You will find Him in a stable." Suddenly, many angels appeared in the sky. They were all praising God. When they left, the shepherds went to Bethlehem to see Jesus. They found Him and began praising God. They told many about the birth of Jesus. Sometime later, Jesus was visited by three wise men who brought Him expensive gifts. They also praised God for sending a Savior. Adapted from Luke 2: 1-12.

Mark 12:30 - Love the Lord your God with all your heart, soul, mind, and strength (adapted).

My Gift to God is Me

I _____ give myself to God as a gift. I will love Him with all of my heart, soul, mind, and strength.

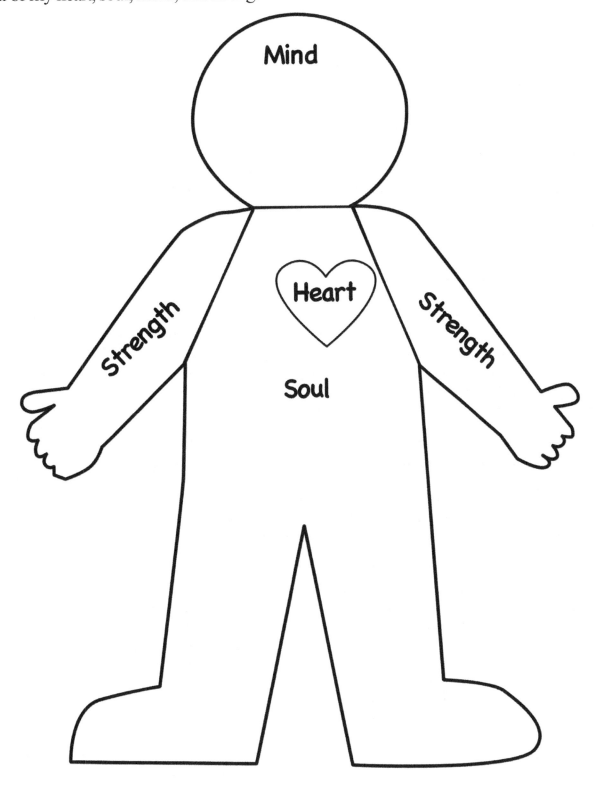

Robinson and Johnson

Devotional 7

Having Faith in God Makes us Happy

Materials needed - magazine, 8 1/2 X 11 sheet of paper, a cup for each family member, carbonated liquid, a pitcher of water, and a happy face.

Scripture - Hebrews 11:6 - *We must have faith in God to please Him (adapted).*

Goal - We will understand that having faith in God makes Him happy and us happy.

I am not happy. + I have faith in God. = God is happy and I am happy.

Object lesson - Before the devotional begins, give each family member a small cup. Have a pitcher of tap water and a bottle of your family's favorite carbonated drink available. Talk about the things in life that make us happy. God knows what is best for us. When we have faith in Him to fill our lives with good things, He does. Having faith in God brings happiness.

Pour each member of your family a small amount of non-carbonated water in each glass. Have them take a sip. Say, "This water is what life tastes like when we don't have faith in God. Have your family members finish drinking all the liquid in their cups. Now pour a small amount of carbonated fluid in each family member's cup. Have them each take a sip. Compare the two liquids. Tell your family, "The bubbles in the carbonated liquid are like our faith. Our faith bubbles up inside us and brings us happiness and pleases God."

Vocabulary development - Introduce the vocabulary words to the family. Talk about the meaning of each word. Acting out the meaning of the words through mime and gestures increases the understanding of the concepts.

> **Faith** - believing in something you can't see or feel
> **Happiness** - my feelings feel good
> **Temple** - a place for people to gather to worship God

Bible Lesson - Look at the scripture card and point out the features of the picture while you read the Bible story out loud. Read the scripture out loud and have your family members repeat it several times. Color the scripture card together. Discuss the following with your family.

- What did Hannah pray for?
- What did she tell God she would do if He gave her a son?
- How did Hannah show that she had faith in God?
- What does Samuel mean?
- Did Hannah honor her promise to God?

Application - Having faith in God makes us happy. When we have faith, we don't have to be unhappy because we know God wants what is best for us. We know he will give us what is best for us. Take an 8 X 11 ½ sheet of paper and fold in down the middle to make two columns. Above one column write "Wants" and above the other column write "Needs". Assist your family members to understand the difference between wants and needs. Needs are things we must have like water, food, shelter, and clothing. Wants are everything else. Encourage each family member to look through a magazine and cut out a picture of something they want and need. Glue the pictures on the appropriate side of the paper. Talk about their selections. Say, "We can have faith that God will provide for us all that we need. We can have faith that God sometimes gives us what we want if it is good for us."

Review the scripture with your family often.

Family Declaration: We declare that every day our faith in God brings us happiness. Our happiness is not determined by our circumstances, it's determined by our faith. We will trust in Him and not lean on our understanding. Throughout our life we need to acknowledge God and He will direct our paths. When we trust in God nothing can stop us. If God is for us who can be against us? This is our declaration!

Champion: I declare that every day my faith in God brings me happiness. I will choose to be happy no matter how hard things get. I know God is for me. He is on my side. I will wake up every morning with a smile on my face knowing that I am a child of God! This is my declaration!

Family Prayer - Read the family prayer together.

   Thank You God for giving us everything we need and sometimes You give us the things we want. Please help us to remember to be happy no matter what we have. Thank you for giving us the greatest gift, Jesus. Amen.

Hannah is Happy
Scripture Card

Hebrews 11:6 - We must have faith in God to please Him (adapted).

Hannah is Happy
Scripture Card

Hannah was a married woman who didn't have a child. She often went to the temple to talk to God and ask Him to give her a child. In the Bible days, married women without children were considered cursed or not favored by God. More than anything Hannah wanted a child. Hannah asked God for a child often. One day God promised He would answer her prayers and give her a son. She had faith that God would keep His promise so she was very happy. She told God that if He gave her a child, she would give the child back to God and he would serve God all his life.

When Hannah's son was born she named him Samuel which means "God hears". When Samuel was old enough, Hannah took him to the temple and there he served the Lord by helping Eli the priest.

Every year Hannah and her husband came to see Samuel at the temple. Each year she brought him a special robe she made for him. God was especially good to Hannah. He gave her three more sons and two daughters. Adapted from I Samuel 1:1-24.

Hebrews 11:6 - We must have faith in God to please Him (adapted).

Sad and Comfortable Faces

Please color, cut out, and glue the faces onto a craft stick.

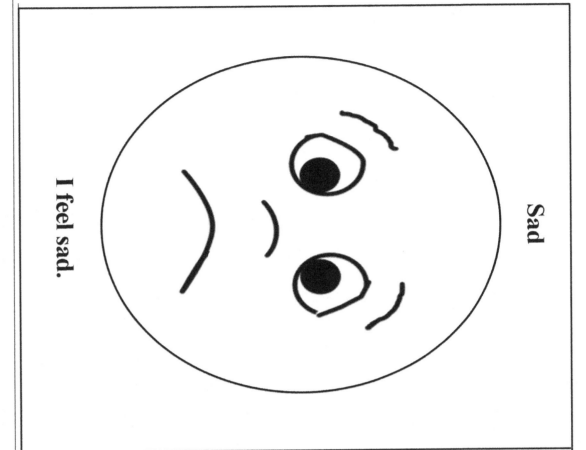

Sad

I feel sad.

Comfortable

My feelings feel ok.

Robinson and Johnson

Devotional 8

Sadness

Materials needed - flashlight, sad and comfortable faces

Scripture - 2 Samuel 22:29 - *You are my lamp, O Lord; the Lord turns my darkness into light.*
Psalms 34: 18 - *The Lord is close to the brokenhearted and saves those who are crushed in spirit.*

Goal - We will understand that when we are sad we can think about God and be comfortable.

I feel sad.   +   I think of God's love for me.   =   I am comfortable.

Object lesson - Tell your family, "Sadness feels like we are in a dark and lonely place. Sadness means you are unhappy." Show your family the sad face. Turn off the lights and turn on a flash light and read the scriptures to your family. Say, "When I am sad and feel like everything is dark, I know God will help me. He brings light into my life. His Word says, 'You are my lamp, O Lord; The Lord turns my darkness into light' (2 Samuel 22:29). When I feel like my heart is breaking, I know He will save me. The Bible says, 'The Lord is close to the brokenhearted and saves those who are crushed in spirit"(Psalm 34:18). Turn off the flashlight and turn on the lights. Say, "When Jesus is in our lives, He brings light to us and we feel comfortable again." Show your family the comfortable face.

Vocabulary development - Introduce the vocabulary words to the family. Talk about the meaning of each word. Acting out the meaning of the words through mime and gestures increases the understanding of the concepts.

Sad - unhappy
Heartbroken - very unhappy, your heart feels heavy in your chest
Lamp - object that gives light
Comfortable - my feelings feel ok

Bible Lesson - Look at the scripture card and point out the features of the picture while you read the Bible story out loud. Read the scripture out loud and have your family members repeat it several times. After you read the Bible story, discuss the following questions with your family. Color the scripture card together.

1. Who was not a friend of Jesus?
2. What did Judas do to Jesus?
3. Why did Jesus pray?
4. What did Jesus want the disciples to do with Him?

Application - Review the following equation. Say, "What we think, affects how we feel, and how we feel influences how we act." Show your family the diagram below.

Our Thoughts $\longrightarrow$ Our Feelings $\longrightarrow$ Our Actions

Continue with, "There are many things that make us sad. We can feel sad when the people we love are sick, or we feel like we have no friends, or we lose something we like." Encourage your family members to share about something that makes them sad.

Say, "When we are sad our bodies can feel a certain way. Sometimes when we feel sad we cry, or we can't sleep, or we can't eat, or we eat too much, or our stomach hurts, or we have a headache. We can change the way our bodies feel when we change what we are thinking. We can think about how much God loves us and how He will never leave us. We can think about His love being a great light in our lives. This will help us feel comfortable again. Comfortable is a good feeling. It means my feelings feel OK." Show your family the comfortable face. Say, "Some other things we can do to help us feel comfortable are as follows:

- Pray to God for help. We can say, 'God please help us feel comfortable.'
- Read, think about, and memorize God's Word.
- Praise God for all the good things in our lives.
- Talk to an adult or friend about how we are feeling.
- Do something we like to do.
- Listen to worship music."

Encourage your family members to add to this list and post the list in a place where family members can see it.

Review the scripture verse with your family often.

Family Declaration: We declare we are living every day like it's a gift from God. His plans for us are good and not evil. We're not defeated, complaining or focused on the negative. Instead we will meditate on the good things God has done in our lives, thanking Him for what He's given us. This is our declaration!

Champion: I declare today is a gift from God. His plans for me are good. I will not focus on what makes me sad, I will focus on God's Word and what He says about me. God says I am strong, healthy, beautiful, smart, and an overcomer. This is my declaration!

Family Prayer – Read the family prayer together.

Dear God,

Thank You for always being with us. Help us, when we feel sad, to think about Your love and protection. Thank You for making us feel comfortable through Your Word, the Bible. Amen.

No More Sadness
Scripture Card

2 Samuel 22:29 - You are my lamp, O Lord; the Lord turns my darkness into light.

Psalms 34: 18 - The Lord is close to the brokenhearted and saves those who are crushed in spirit.

No More Sadness
Scripture Card

Jesus was having dinner with all His disciples. Everyone was having a good time when Jesus said, "One of you at this table is not my true friend."

After Jesus said this Judas, the disciple, ran away. Earlier in the day, Judas told the Roman leader that he would show him where Jesus was and who He was if the Roman leader gave him some money. The Romans wanted to arrest and hurt Jesus because He said He was the Son of God and they didn't believe Him. Judas told the Roman leader that the person he kissed on the cheek would be Jesus.

Jesus was sad. He knew the Romans were going to hurt Him so he wanted to spend some time in prayer. He asked His most trusted disciples to go with Him to pray. Jesus had a special place to pray. It was His sanctuary. It was in a garden. He left the disciples at the opening of a garden and He went deep into the garden to talk to God. After an hour of praying, Jesus came to the opening of the garden. He saw all the disciples were asleep. This made Him feel alone and sad. He did this two more times.

After the third time, He came out to check on the disciples. Jesus said, "Couldn't you stay awake one hour to pray with me?" As Jesus was saying this, Judas and the Roman guards came to Him. Judas kissed Him on the cheek and the soldiers took Jesus away. Adapted from Matthew 26:36-46.

2 Samuel 22:29 – You are my lamp, O Lord; the Lord turns my darkness into light.

Psalms 34: 18 – The Lord is close to the brokenhearted and saves those who are crushed in spirit.

Devotional 9

When I am Sad, I Can Trust in God to Help Me.

Materials needed - 1 brown paper bag, a blind fold, common household items that are not sharp, and sad and comfortable faces.

Scripture - Hebrews 13:8 - *Jesus Christ is the same yesterday, today, and forever .*

Goal - We will learn how to turn our sadness into comfort when we remind ourselves about God's positive and unchanging characteristics.

I feel sad. + I have faith that God will help me. = I am comfortable.

Object lesson - Place several common household items into a large bag that is not transparent. There should be at least one item per family member placed in the bag. Tell your family, "We are going to play a guessing game! We are going to guess what objects are in this bag by following these steps. (Demonstrate the steps as you say them.) First, put your hand inside the bag and select one of the objects. Don't remove your hand from the bag. Next, while you are holding the object, tell us what you think the object is. Last, remove the object from the bag so we all can see if your guess was correct." After each family member has had an opportunity to play the game say,

- " Faith is believing in something you can't see.
- It is by faith that we know what an object is without seeing it.
- While we can't see God, our past experiences with God help us to have faith in Him."

Even when we are sad, we can have faith God will help us be comfortable again because that is what He always does."

Vocabulary development - Introduce the vocabulary words to the family. Talk about the meaning of each word. Acting out the meaning of the words through mime and gestures increases the understanding of the concepts.

    Faith - believing in something you can't see
    Forever - something that never ends
    Comfortable - my feelings feel good

Bible Lesson - Look at the scripture card and point out the features of the picture while you read the Bible story out loud. Read the scripture out loud and have your family members repeat it several times. After you read the Bible story, discuss the following questions with your family. Color the scripture card together.

1. What did Lazarus and his sisters Mary and Martha believe about Jesus?
2. What happened to Lazarus?
3. How did Jesus feel about what happened to Lazarus?
4. What did Jesus do for Lazarus?
5. How did Mary, Martha, and Lazarus feel when Lazarus rose from the dead?

Application - Have the family members look at the *Faith Self-talk Chart*. Say, "We all have characteristics. Characteristics are the way we act. God has characteristics. Look at the pictures on the *Faith Self-Talk Chart* that represent some of His characteristics. The chart shows that He always acts the same. He is our protector. He loves us, and He keeps His promises. We will remember these things when we are sad so we can be comfortable again." Encourage family members to give personal examples of when they experienced God's protection, love, and His ability to keep His promises.

Say, "At one time or another most people talk to themselves. Faith self-talk is like talking to yourself about the greatest of God. Look at the *Faith Self-Talk Chart*. Notice that on the chart there are two columns and four rows. The first column is entitled, 'What is happening to cause me to feel sad?' Look at the second column. It says, 'Statement of Faith'. Look at the picture in the box. The picture is entitled, 'God is my Protector'. In the box across from this picture, write down or draw a picture of some of the experiences the family members have had where God protected them. Repeat this procedure for the next three boxes. Faith self-talk is making statements about who God is and what He can do for you and others. Practice using faith self-talk often."

Review the scripture verse with your family often.

Family Declaration: We declare that whatever we face in life, we will not let circumstances determine our outcome. We will live in the vision and not the problem. We know this situation is not final. God is preparing us for something greater to come. Our faith is taking us higher. We are coming out better than we were before. This is our declaration!

Champion: I declare that whatever I face, I will have faith in God. I know what I am going through is not final. God is preparing me to do great things. My faith in God is taking me higher. I am coming out better than I was before. This is my declaration!

Family Prayer – Read the family prayer together.

Dear God,

Thank You for always being the same. Help us to grow our faith in You by practicing faith self-talk. Thank You for helping us to be comfortable in any situation knowing that You protect us, keep Your promises, You are always with us, and love us. Amen.

From Sadness to Happiness
Scripture Card

Hebrews 13:8 - Jesus Christ is the same yesterday, today and forever.

From Sadness to Happiness
Scripture Card

Lazarus and his sisters, Martha and Mary, were close friends of Jesus. They believed that Jesus was the son of God. They knew He could heal people.

One day Martha sent a message to Jesus to come and see Lazarus because he was very sick and dying. Jesus didn't come right away, and then Lazarus died. Martha and Mary were very sad. Four days after Lazarus died, Jesus came to the city where Martha and Mary lived. Martha ran out to meet Him and told Him that Lazarus was dead. Martha took Jesus to Mary. When Mary saw Him, she fell at His feet and cried because she missed her brother so much. All three of them were very sad.

Martha and Mary took Jesus to the place where Lazarus was buried. It was a cave with a stone covering the opening. Jesus asked them to roll away the stone. Jesus prayed to God. He had faith in God and asked God for a miracle. He said, "Lazarus, come out!" Lazarus came out of the cave. He was alive. It was a miracle. Mary, Martha, an Lazarus thanked Jesus for performing the miracle.

There are situations in life that can cause us to feel sad, but we know that God can turn those situations into something good. Adapted from John 11: 1-43

Hebrews 13:8 – Jesus Christ is the same yesterday, today and forever.

When I Am Sad, I Can Trust God to Help Me   Devotional 9

Faith Self-Talk Chart

Look at the statements of faith and the pictures on the right hand side of the chart. Think of a situation where the faith statement would apply. Write down a brief statement or draw a picture that represents the situation on the left hand side of the chart.

What is happening to cause me to feel sad?	Statement of Faith
	 **God is my protector.**
	 **God keeps His promises.**
	 **God is always with us.**
	♡ **God is love.**

Devotional 10

When I am Sad, I Can Praise God

Materials needed - enough sunglasses for everyone, picture of Jesus (found in devotional 6), sad and comfortable faces.

Scripture - Psalms 42:5 - *When I am sad, I will praise God my Savior! (adapted).*

Goal - We will learn how to turn our sad feelings into those of comfort when we praise God for all His blessings in our lives.

I am sad.   +   I praise God.   =   I am comfortable.

Object lesson - Say, "There are many things in our lives that make us feel sad." Show your family the sad face. Continue with, "Some things that make us feel sad are when someone in our family is sick, you lose something important to you, when someone or something dies, or when we feel like we have no friends. Sadness is like wearing sunglasses inside the house. It makes everything look dark." Have your family members put on a pair of glasses and hold up a picture of Jesus. Tell them: "Looking at Jesus through sunglasses makes Him harder to see. When we are sad, the Bible says the best way to get comfortable again is to praise God for all of the good things in our lives." Show your family the comfortable face. Remind them that comfortable means my feelings feel ok. Say, "When we praise and thank God for loving us, protecting us, always being with us, and for always keeping His promises it's like taking off the sunglasses." Have everyone take off their sunglasses. Say to them, "Things around us start to look brighter when we praise God. We can see Jesus more clearly and understand how much He loves us."

Vocabulary development - Introduce the vocabulary words to the family. Talk about the meaning of each word. Acting out the meaning of the words through mime and gestures increases the understanding of the concepts.

Praise - give thanks, admire God, talk about His greatness
Comfortable - my feelings feel good
Sad - grief, unhappy
Savior - someone who saves us from harm

Bible Lesson - Look at the scripture card and point out the features of the picture while you read the Bible story out loud. Read the scripture out loud and have your family members repeat it several times. Color the scripture card together. Discuss the following with your family.

- What is leprosy?
- How many lepers were there?
- What did the lepers want from Jesus?
- What did Jesus do for the lepers?
- How many of the ten lepers came back to thank Jesus?

Application - Say, "When we worship and praise God, He can turn our sadness into feelings of comfort." Discuss the many ways to worship and praise God with your family. Model the different ways you can worship and praise God. Tell your family the following:

- We can worship God by praying. Praying is simply talking to God.

- Praise God by taking the letters in your first name and finding words or phrases to describe God using those letters. For example if your name is "Sandra", you could thank God for being; **S**uper, **A**mazing, **N**ear us always, **D**ynamic, **R**ighteous, **A**wesome.

- We can praise God by reading the Bible or listening to scriptures.

- Worship God through singing praise songs or listening to them.

- Praise God by doing a dance for Him.

Practice praising God with your family. Review the scripture verse with your family often.

Family Declaration: We declare to praise God in every situation. When we feel sad or happy our response will be the same. We know our praise is changing the atmosphere in our circumstances. God is working behind the scenes to bring us out better than we were before. This is our declaration!

Champion: I declare to praise God even when I'm sad. I will not let my feelings stop me from praising God. I know my praise is changing my situation. God is working to make me better than I was before. This is my declaration!

Family Prayer – Read the family prayer together.

Dear God,

Thank You for being with us always. Help us when we feel sad to praise You. Thank You for sending Your Son Jesus to die for our sins so that we could be with You forever. Help us to be comfortable when we remember Your love for us. Amen.

The Ten Lepers
Scripture Card

Psalms 42: 5 – When I am sad, I will praise God my Savior! (adapted)

The Ten Lepers
Scripture Card

One day while Jesus was walking along a highway, He saw a group of lepers off in the distance. A leper is a person who has a disease called leprosy. Leprosy is a disease that causes people to break out in sores all over their bodies. It is highly contagious; therefore, individuals with leprosy in Jesus' time were isolated from those without the disease. These lepers were very sad. They were unable to live with their families because they had the disease.

The ten lepers asked Jesus to heal them. Jesus healed them and told them to show themselves to the priest. In those days, the priest was someone who could tell if a person had leprosy or not.

As the lepers left to go see the priest, they noticed their sores were gone. They were so happy. Suddenly, one of them stopped and went running back to find Jesus. When he saw Jesus, he began thanking and praising Him for healing him. Jesus noticed that he was the only man who came back to thank Him. We must thank God every day for who He is and how much He loves us and others. Adapted from Luke 17:11-19.

Psalms 42: 5 - When I am sad, I will praise God my Savior! (adapted)

Devotional 11

I am in God's Family

Materials needed - hard-boiled egg, black fine tipped permanent marker, sad and comfortable faces

Scripture - John 3:16 - *God loves us so much that He gave His Son Jesus to die for our sins. If we believe in Him, we will be part of God's family forever (adapted).*

Goal - We will learn that not being part of God's family makes us sad. We will learn how to be part of God's family which brings us comfort and peace.

I have sinned and I am sad. + I ask for forgiveness. = God forgives me, so I feel comfortable.

Object lesson - Tell your family, "When we are born, we look like this." Hold up the egg. Continue with, "We are clean and white inside. As we grow, we do a lot of good things, such as sharing our things with others and helping others. As we grow, we also say or think things that are selfish and hurtful towards others. We hurt others by calling them names and hitting them. These things are called sins. Sinning often makes us sad." Show your family the picture of the sad face. Say, "Let's name some sins. As you say these sins, I am going to write them on this egg." Write the name of the sins on the egg with permanent marker. Show the students the egg. It should be covered with words. Say, "The shell of the egg is covered with sins and looks dirty. When we believe that Jesus is God's Son and ask God to forgive us of our sins, we can be clean again just like this egg." Peel the egg and show the students the egg. Say, "We can be comfortable again." Show your family the comfortable face." Say the scripture together.

Vocabulary development - Introduce the vocabulary words to the family. Talk about the meaning of each word. Acting out the meaning of the words through mime and gestures increases the understanding of the concepts.

> **Sin -** doing the wrong thing, not following God's rules
> **Sad -** grief, unhappy
> **Praise -** to gives thanks, admiration, or approval
> **Comfortable -** my feelings feel ok
> **Savior -** someone who saves us from harm, Jesus is our Savior

Bible Lesson - Look at the scripture card and point out the features of the picture while you read the Bible story out loud. Read the scripture out loud and have your family members repeat it several times. Color the scripture card together. Discuss the following with your family.

- What has God planned for all of us?
- Since God is perfect, what can't He look at?
- What did God send Jesus to do?
- What do we need to do to be part of God's family?

Application - Say, "If you would like to be a part of God's family and want God to be with you all the time, ask Him to forgive you of your sins. If you have already done this, you can still pray the following prayer with us to remind yourself of your decision to be a part of God's family. Let's pray this prayer together."

Say the prayer one phrase at a time and have your family members repeat it.

> Dear Heavenly Father,
> I believe Jesus is Your Son.
> I believe Jesus died on the cross for my sins.
> I believe that Jesus rose again and He is alive in heaven.
> Please forgive me for all the things I have done wrong.
> Please come into my heart and help me love You and others.
> Amen.

Every day this week thank God for loving you enough to give His Son as a sacrifice for your sins. Tell others about God's love for you and them.

Review the scripture verse with your family often.

Family Declaration: We declare that we are a part of God's family. Through salvation we inherit all of God's benefits. Because we are His children, He is going before us making crooked paths straight. We are growing stronger, healthier, and wiser because we have the DNA of almighty God living within us. Nothing can separate us from the love of God. This is our declaration!

Champion: I declare I am a part of God's family. Because I've given my life to God, I receive all of his blessings. I am growing stronger, healthier, and wiser because God lives in me. Nothing can separate me from God's love. This is my declaration!

Family Prayer – Read the family prayer together.

Dear God,

Thank You God for saving us by sending Your Son, Jesus, who died on the cross for our sins. Help us learn to accept Your forgiveness and try not to sin again. Thank You for forgiving our sins when we ask You to. This makes us feel comfortable again. Amen.

Jesus Died for All of Us
Scripture Card

John 3:16 – God loves us so much, that He gave His Son Jesus to die for our sins. If we believe in Him, we will be part of God's family forever (adapted).

Jesus Died for All of Us
Scripture Card

God planned for all of us to be in His family forever. He has always loved us. There was a problem with this plan. It is called sin.

Sometimes we do things that are wrong. The things we do wrong are called sins. Since God is perfect, He can't look at sin. God can't be around us when we sin. God loves us and it makes Him sad not to be around us so He found a way to fix this problem. He sent His one and only son, Jesus, to the earth to show us how to live our lives and die for our sins.

Jesus taught us many things. He healed many people, performed many miracles, and loved us all with a perfect love. Jesus also took away our sins by dying a painful death on the cross. He took our sins as His own and died. Our sins were buried with Him. When Jesus died, his friends and family were very, very sad. They didn't have to be sad for very long because three days later, Jesus came back to life. He had conquered death! He now was without sin. He showed Himself to his friends and his disciples.

To be in God's family forever, we have to believe that Jesus is God's Son, that He died on the cross for our sins, and that He rose again on the third day. We must ask for forgiveness for all our sins.

When we do this, God forgives us, and we become sparkling clean on the inside, like the white part of the egg. We become part of God's family forever!

John 3:16 - God loves us so much that He gave His Son Jesus to die for our sins. If we believe in Him, we will be part of God's family forever (adapted).

Devotional 12

How to Stay Right with God

Materials needed - bandage and sad and comfortable faces

Scripture - I John 1:9 - *If we tell God that we have sinned, He will forgive us of our sins and make us clean again (adapted).*

Goal - We will learn that when we sin we are sad, but when we repent of our sin we feel comfortable again.

I have sinned and I am sad. + I can repent. = I am alright with God, so I am comfortable.

Object lesson - Show a bandage to your family. Ask them, "What is a bandage used for?" The answer would be that it's used to keep a cut clean. Discuss how it feels when you have a small cut. Ask your family, "Why should we clean and bandage the cut?" The answer is that it heals faster. Tell them, "When the cut is healed, it's like it didn't happen. The skin grows over the cut and the cut is erased."

Say, "When we do something wrong like lying, stealing, or hurting others, it is like having a cut on the inside. It hurts and makes us sad because we know we have done something wrong. We have sinned." Show your family the sad face. Continue with, "We can clean the inside like we clean the outside. The first thing we need to do to clean the inside is to tell God we did something wrong. We can put a bandage on the cut on the inside by asking God to forgive us and cover us with His love. This is called repentance. Repentance is a way of cleaning our spiritual cuts and being alright with God. Once we are alright with God, we can be comfortable again." Show your family the comfortable face.

Vocabulary development - Introduce the vocabulary words to the family. Talk about the meaning of each word. Acting out the meaning of the words through mime and gestures increases the understanding of the concepts.

> **Repent** - tell God you have sinned and ask for His forgiveness
> **Commandment** - God's law
> **Forgive** - to stop being angry with someone who has done something to hurt you

Bible Lesson - Look at the scripture card and point out the features of the picture while you read the Bible story out loud. Read the scripture out loud and have your family members repeat it several times. Color the scripture card together. Discuss the following with your family.

- What did the people of Israel do in Egypt?
- What did God do for them?
- Who did God give the Ten Commandments to?
- What are the Ten Commandments?
- Why is it important to follow God's law?

Application - Every day we make good and bad choices. When we refuse to follow God's laws or commandments, it makes us feel sad. We must ask God to forgive us. This is called repenting.

When God forgives us we feel comfortable. When we are forgiven, we are clean inside. When we repent, we try not to do the same thing again. We try to make good choices.

Look at the **Ten Commandment Cards**. Talk about the commandments and color the cards together. Cut out the cards, punch a hole in them, and put them on a ring so you can take them everywhere you go to remind you of God's laws. When we follow God's laws, He is happy and so are we.

Follow the steps on the **Repentance Conversation Cards** to help you feel comfortable after you have sinned. Encourage your family members to share when they sinned and repented.

Review the scripture verse with your family often.

Family Declaration: We declare there is no condemnation for those who believe. We can release guilt, hurt, and unforgiveness because we know when we ask, God will always forgive. We are letting go of our past and looking forward to our future. God's Word says, that the glory of this house will be greater than our former house. We are expecting God's glory to shine down on us greater than ever before. This is our declaration!

Champion: I declare that when I ask, God will always forgive me. I am letting go of anything bad, and looking forward to my future. I am expecting God's goodness to shine down on me greater than ever before. This is my declaration!

Family Prayer – Read the family prayer together.

Dear God,

Thank You for forgiving us when we ask You to. Please help us do the things You want us to do. Thank You for sending Your Son Jesus to die for our sins so we could be with You forever. Amen.

Moses and the Ten Commandments
Scripture Card

1 John 1:9 – If we tell God that we have sinned, He will forgive us of our sins and make us clean again (adapted).

Moses and the Ten Commandments
Scripture Card

After God brought the people of Israel out of their slavery in Egypt, they traveled through the desert. After several months, God had them camp in front of Mount Sinai. God asked Moses to come to the top of the mountain so He could speak to Moses about how His people should live. God wanted His people to do the right thing so they could have a great life.

At the top of Mount Sinai, God gave Moses specific laws the people who loved God should follow. The new laws were called the Ten Commandments.

The Ten Commandments

1. Love God more than you love anyone else.
2. Make God the most important thing in your life.
3. Always say God's name with respect.
4. Honor God by spending Sunday resting and thinking about Him.
5. Love, respect, and obey your parents.
6. Never hurt others.
7. Be faithful to your husband or wife.
8. Don't take things that aren't yours.
9. Always tell the truth.
10. Be happy with what you have.

When we follow the Ten Commandments, good things happen in our lives. When we do follow the laws of God, we can enjoy all the wonderful things God has for us. Adapted from Exodus 20:1-17.

1 John 1:9 - If we tell God that we have sinned, He will forgive us of our sins and make us clean again (adapted).

The Ten Commandments Bible Cards

Discuss the Ten Commandments with the students. Give examples of each commandment.
Show the students the picture that corresponds with each commandment as you teach.

1. Love God more than you love anything else.

2. Make God the most important thing in your life.

#1

3. Always say God's name with respect.

I only say God's name when I am praying.

4. Honor God by spending Sunday resting and thinking about Him.

The Ten Commandments Bible Cards

The Ten Commandments Bible Cards

The Ten Commandments Bible Cards

The Ten Commandments Bible Cards

The Ten Commandments Bible Cards

Discuss the Ten Commandments with the students. Give examples of each commandment.
Show the students the picture that corresponds with each commandment as you teach.

5. Love, respect, and obey your parents.

6. Never hurt others.

7. Be faithful to your husband or wife.

8. Don't take things that belong to others without asking. This is stealing.

The Ten Commandments Bible Cards

The Ten Commandments Bible Cards

The Ten Commandments Bible Cards

The Ten Commandments Bible Cards

The Ten Commandments Bible Cards

Discuss the Ten Commandments with the students. Give examples of each commandment.
Show the students the picture that corresponds with each commandment as you teach.

9. **Always tell the truth.**

I will tell the truth.

10. **Be happy with what you have.**

I am happy building.

The Ten Commandments Bible Cards

1 John 1:9 - If we tell God that we have sinned, He will forgive us of our sins and make us clean again (adapted).

The Ten
Commandments
Bible Cards

The Ten
Commandments
Bible Cards

The Ten
Commandments
Bible Cards

The Ten
Commandments
Bible Cards

Repentance Conversation Cards

Use the *Repentance Conversation Cards* as you model how to repent and ask for forgiveness.

1 I did something wrong. I feel sad. Yesterday, I took something that wasn't mine.

CONVERSATION CARDS
Repentance

2 I can ask God to forgive me. I can pray, "God please forgive me and help me do the right thing."

CONVERSATION CARDS
Repentance

3 I can fix the mistake. I apologize and return the item I took.

CONVERSATION CARDS
Repentance

4 I can decide not to do it again. I can pray, "God please help me follow Your commandments."

CONVERSATION CARDS
Repentance

Devotional 13

My Sins Bring Sadness

Materials needed - 3 pieces of blank white computer paper, marker, and a large bag of jelly beans (black, red, white, yellow, green), and sad and comfortable faces

Scripture - Romans 10:9 - *If you say out loud that Jesus is Lord, and believe in your heart that God raised Him from the dead, you shall be saved .*

Goal - We will understand that when we have faith in God, He is happy and we are happy.

Jesus died on the cross for my sins and I am sad. + Jesus rose from the dead and is alive. = I feel happy.

Object lesson - You have three sheets of blank white computer paper. On the first piece of paper write the word "Us" and draw a few stick figures representing your family. On another sheet of paper write the word "God" and draw a heart on it. On the last sheet of paper, write the word "Jesus" and draw a bridge on it. Place the paper with "God" written on it close to the paper with "Us" written on it. Have a family member stand on the piece of paper that says "Us". Say, "God created us to have a close relationship with Him. He wanted us to be close to Him always." Have a family member step back and forth from the piece of paper that says "Us" to the piece of paper that says "God" a few times to illustrate the concept.

Tell your family, "Sin separates us from God. Sinning is choosing not to follow God's laws. God can't look at sin. When we sin, we can't be with God." As you talk, move the piece of paper with "God" written on it further away from the piece of paper with "Us" written on it. Move the paper far enough away so that the family members could not safely step from paper to paper. Say, "As you can see there needs to be a bridge to help us get to God and Jesus is that bridge." Make sure the paper with "Jesus" written on it touches both the "Us" and the "God" paper. Tell your family, "When Jesus died on the cross he paid the price for our sin. When we ask for forgiveness for our sins, Jesus forgives us. When God looks at us He sees Jesus who never sinned. We can be happy because through Jesus we are able to have a relationship with God. We have a special day each year to remember Jesus' sacrifice on the cross and his resurrection. It is called Easter." (adapted from Hawkes, 2014).

Vocabulary development - Introduce the vocabulary words to the family. Talk about the meaning of each word. Acting out the meaning of the words through mime and gestures increases the understanding of the concepts.

    Tomb - a place for the burial of a dead body
    Resurrection- when Jesus rose from the dead after dying on the cross for our sins

Bible Lesson - Look at the scripture card and point out the features of the picture while you read the Bible story out loud. Read the scripture out loud and have your family members repeat it several times. Color the scripture card together. Discuss the following with your family:

- Why did Jesus die on the cross?
- Where did they bury him?
- Who came to Jesus' tomb? What did they find?
- If we accept Jesus as our Savior, what happens to us when we die?

Application - A bag of jelly beans can help us remember Biblical truths about salvation. Give each family member one jelly bean of each of the following colors: black, red, white, yellow, and green. Talk about what each color represents and read the scripture associated with it. Read and discuss with your family the Salvation Jelly Bean Chart. Share the Jelly Bean Salvation Plan with others.

The Salvation Jelly Bean Chart

Black - The black jelly bean represents sin. Sin is disobeying God's commandments.
Romans 3:23 - *We all have sinned and fallen short of the Glory of God.*

Red-The red jelly bean represents the blood that Jesus lost when He died on the cross for our sins. Through His sacrifice we are able to have a relationship with God.
Ephesians 1:7 - *God is so rich in kindness and grace that He purchased our freedom with the blood of His Son and forgave our sins* (New Living Translation).

White- The white jelly bean represents how we feel on the inside when we are forgiven. If we tell Him our sins, we can depend on Him to forgive us of our sins.
I John 1:9 - *If we tell Him our sins, we can depend on Him to forgive us of our sins (adapted).*

Yellow- The yellow jelly bean reminds us that Jesus is the light and through Him we can have a relationship with God.
John 14:6 - *Jesus said to him, "I am the way, and the truth, and the life. No one comes to the Father except through me."*

Green –The green jelly bean represents our need to grow and mature in our relationship with God and others.
2 Peter 3:18 - *But grow in the grace and knowledge of our Lord and Savior Jesus Christ* (New International Version). Adapted from Creative Youth Ideas, 2014.

Review the scriptures with your family often.

Family Declaration: We declare to honor God by making good choices. Every good decision we make, we know He will bless. We will stay away from negative situations and watch God give us positive results. We will begin to heal when we let go of past hurts, forgive those who've wronged us, and forgive ourselves for our mistakes. Our best days are in front of us. This is our declaration!

Champion: I declare to honor God by making good choices. I will stay away from negative things that will make me sad. I will let go of past hurts and watch God do amazing things in my life. My best days are in front of me. This is my declaration!

Family Prayer- Read the family prayer together.

Dear God, Thank You Jesus for dying on the cross for our sins. Please help us to always remember that Your sacrifice makes it possible for us to have a relationship with You. Thank You for giving us the courage to share Your love with others. Amen.

Jesus is Alive
Scripture Card

Romans 10:9 - If you say out loud that Jesus is Lord, and believe in your heart that God raised Him from the dead, you shall be saved (adapted).

Jesus is Alive
Scripture Card

We have all sinned. Jesus died on the cross for our sins. After Jesus died on the cross, some Roman soldiers placed His body in a tomb. They rolled a very large rock over the opening of the tomb so no one could remove His body. On the morning of the third day after Jesus died, there was a mighty earthquake. The stone across the tomb was rolled away. Jesus Christ walked out of the tomb alive.

Later that morning, Mary, the mother of Jesus, and Mary Magdalene went to visit the tomb of Jesus. As they approached the tomb they saw an angel sitting on top of the stone. They were afraid. The angel said to the women, "Do not be afraid. I know you are looking for Jesus, but He isn't here. He has risen from the dead just as He said He would! Come and see for yourself that the tomb is empty. If you want to find Jesus, He's on His way to Galilee." The women ran to the road that led to Galilee to see if they could find Jesus. As they were running down the path they turned a corner, and there was Jesus. The ladies fell at His feet and worshiped Him. They were so happy to see Jesus. Many days later Jesus went up to heaven to be with His father. Jesus will one day come back to take everyone who accepts Him as their Savior to live with Him in heaven forever. Adapted from Matthew 27 and 28.

Romans 10:9 - If you say out loud that Jesus is Lord, and believe in your heart that God raised Him from the dead, you shall be saved (adapted).

My Sins Bring Sadness   Devotional 13

The Salvation Jelly Bean Chart

A bag of jelly beans can help us remember Biblical truths about salvation. Color the jelly beans. Talk about what each color represents and read the scripture associated with it.

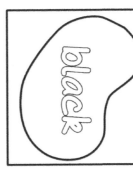

black

red

white

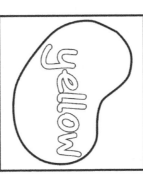

yellow

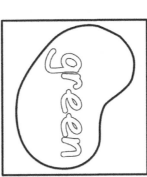

green

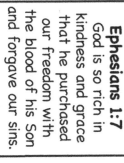

Romans 3:23
We all have sinned and fallen short of the Glory of God.

Ephesians 1:7
God is so rich in kindness and grace that he purchased our freedom with the blood of his Son and forgave our sins.

I John 1:9
If we tell Him our sins, we can depend on Him to forgive us of our sins. He will make our lives clean from all sin (adapted).

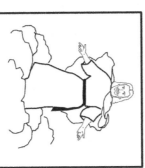

John 14:6
Jesus said to him, "I am the way, and the truth, and the life. No one comes to the Father except through me.

2 Peter 3:18
But grow in the grace and knowledge of our Lord and Savior Jesus Christ.

Fear and Comfortable Faces

Please color, cut out, and glue the faces onto a craft stick.

Fear

I feel afraid.

Comfortable

My feelings feel ok.

Devotional 14

No More Fear

Materials needed - Jacket, long sleeve shirt, hat, scarf, gloves, fear and comfortable faces.

Scripture - Psalm 46:1 - *God is our refuge and strength, always ready to help in times of trouble (adapted NLT).*

Goal - We will learn that when we are afraid we can think about God's protection and be comfortable.

I feel afraid.   +   I think about how God is always with me.   =   I am comfortable.

Object lesson - Come into the room wearing many articles of clothing. Wear several shirts, socks, hats, and scarves. Fan yourself as you tell your family how hot and uncomfortable you are wearing all the items of clothing. Ask your family the following, "I feel hot and uncomfortable in these clothes. What should I do?" Encourage someone to tell you to remove your extra clothing. As you remove some of your extra clothing items say, "Now that I have taken some of my extra clothing off, I feel so much better. I am not hot anymore. I feel comfortable." Show your family the comfortable face. Say, "Sometimes being afraid feels like our bodies are hot. We are very uncomfortable." Show your family the fear face. Say, "God wants us to be comfortable knowing that we have nothing to fear. He will take care of us. We can feel comfortable again." Show your family the comfortable face.

Vocabulary development - Introduce the vocabulary words to the family. Talk about the meaning of each word. Acting out the meaning of the words through mime and gestures increases the understanding of the concepts.

> **Fear** - it is the anticipation of a specific pain or danger
> **Thoughts** - ideas
> **Feelings** - emotions
> **Actions** - what we do
> **Forsake** - to give up on something or someone, desert, abandon, leave

Bible Lesson - Look at the scripture card and point out the features of the picture while you read the Bible story out loud. Read the scripture out loud and have your family members repeat it several times. Color the scripture card together. Discuss the following with your family.

- Who was Elisha?
- Who was fighting God's people?
- Why did the king of Aram want to hurt Elisha?
- Why was the servant of Elisha afraid?
- What did Elisha tell his servant?

Application - Review the following equation with your family. Say, "What we think affects how we feel and how we feel influences how we act." Give examples.

Our Thoughts   ➡   Our Feelings   ➡   Our Actions

Continue with, "We all have things we fear. Some of these things could be a big dog chasing us, we are in a dark room, or someone is trying to hurt us."

Encourage your family members to share about what they fear.

Say, "When we are afraid our bodies can feel a certain way." As you say the following, point to those places on your body. Say, "Sometimes when we are afraid our heart beats faster than it usually does, we breathe faster than normal, sometimes we cry, we feel very hot especially in our face and neck area, or our body shakes. Fear isn't always a bad thing. Fear lets us know that danger is near. It allows us to protect ourselves. Fear can also keep us from doing good things. If we are afraid and want to be comfortable again we can do the following things:

- We can pray, 'God please take our fear away.'
- Think about how much He loves us and that He will protect us.
- We can read the scriptures over and over.
- Praise God for all the good things He has given us.
- Talk to an adult or friend about how we are feeling.
- Do something we like to do.
- Listen to worship music.
- Sing praises to God."

Review the scripture verse with your family often.

Family Declaration: We declare we will not live in fear. In every situation we face we are putting our trust in God's faithfulness. God will never let us down so there is no need to fear. His love never fails. Instead of getting discouraged by what we don't see, we're going to trust God and His timing. At the right time, His promises will come to pass in our lives. This is our declaration!

Champion: I declare I will not live in fear. When I feel afraid, all I have to do is think about God and then I am comfortable. No matter what I face I will put my trust in God's faithfulness. God will never let me down. His love never fails. This is my declaration!

Family Prayer –

Dear God,

Thank you for Your protection, When I am afraid, please help me remember You are always with me. You surround me with Your army of angels. Thank You for helping me feel comfortable in any situation. Amen.

God Protects Me
Scripture Card

Psalm 46:1 - God is our refuge and strength, always ready to help in times of trouble (adapted NLT).

God Protects Me
Scripture Card

The king of Aram was at war with God's people, the Israelites. He had a plan to hide in a certain spot and wait for the army of Israel to pass by so he could surprise it and attack it.

God told Elisha, the prophet, about the king of Aram's plan so he told the leader of Israel's army where the army of Aram was hiding. The ruler of Israel sent soldiers to the place Elisha told him Aram's army was. This greatly angered the king of Aram so he asked several people if they knew who told the king of Israel where Aram's army was hiding. He found out Elisha was the one who told.

The king of Aram was so angry he sent a great army of men riding on horses and in chariots to find Elisha and kill him. The army found out where Elisha was and made plans to kill him. The next day, Elisha woke up and looked out of his window. He saw the king of Aram's army. Elisha's servant stood beside him and looked out the widow at the vast army. He became very afraid. He said, "What are we going to do? This army is going to kill us." Elisha looked at the servant and told him, "Don't be afraid because God's army is much greater and stronger than Aram's army." The servant didn't understand what Elisha was talking about because all he could see was Aram's mighty army. Elisha prayed, "God please open my servant's eyes so he can see your great army." Then God opened the eyes of the servant and he saw the mountains were filled with God's warrior angels riding in chariots of fire. Elisha told the servant he didn't need to be afraid because God was with them always. Both men praised God for His protection and care. Adapted from 2 Kings 6:8-17.

.

Psalm 46:1 - God is our refuge and strength, always ready to help in times of trouble (adapted NLT).

Devotional 15

Increasing My Faith to Overcome My Fear

Materials needed - jar with a lid on it, squeeze ball, and the fear and comfortable faces.

Scripture - Deuteronomy 31:6 - *Be strong and courageous. Do not be afraid because God is with you (adapted).*

Goal - We will learn that we don't need to be afraid because God is with us everywhere we go.

I am afraid to do what God wants me to do.　+　I have faith that God is with me always.
=　God will help me do what He wants me to do.

Object lesson - Dramatically try to open a jar that has been sealed. Ask some of your family members to assist you in opening the jar. Tell them, "You need to build the muscles in your hands in order to open the jar. One way to build your hand muscles is to squeeze a squeeze ball." Demonstrate how to squeeze the squeeze ball. Allow the family members to squeeze the squeeze ball.

Now, try to open the jar. The lid should come off easily since you have exercised your hand muscles. If the jar opens, let your family know that the exercise strengthened your hand muscles and this allowed you to open the lid. If the jar doesn't open, tell your family you need to do more exercises to get the lid off.

Say, "Fear is the opposite of faith. Fear looks like this." Show your family the fear face. Say, "When we are afraid it's hard to do the things God wants us to do like follow His commandments. Building our faith is like building a muscle. The more you use it the stronger it becomes. The greater our faith, the less we fear. The less we fear, the more comfortable we can be in any situation." Show your family the comfortable face.

Continue with, "Let's build our faith muscle by saying the following and believing it. 'God I trust you today. I know you love me and will take care of me. I know you will protect me always. Help me do what you want me to do. Help me build my faith muscle.'"

Vocabulary development - Introduce the vocabulary words to the family. Talk about the meaning of each word. Acting out the meaning of the words through mime and gestures increases the understanding of the concepts.

Discouraged - to give up, not to try
Fear - it is the anticipation of a specific pain or danger
Faith - is believing in something you can't see
Strong - having great physical power and ability

Bible Lesson - Look at the scripture card and point out the features of the picture while you read the Bible story out loud. Read the scripture out loud and have your family members repeat it several times. Color the scripture card together. Discuss the following with your family.

- What did God tell Joshua?
- What was the first city that God told Joshua to conquer?
- What was God's plan for Joshua to take over the city?
- Did the plan work?
- How can we build our faith in God?

Application - Have the family members look at the *Faith Workout Schedule* while you tell them the following, "The activities on the schedule help build our faith muscle." Read the activities on the left side of the chart while you point to the picture that corresponds to the activity. Say, "Let's do some of these activities. These activities will build our faith. When an activity is completed, place a check mark next to the item under the appropriate day of the week." Laminate the schedule so you can reuse it. Place the *Faith Workout Schedule* in a central location in your home where the family members can see it daily.

Review the scripture verse with your family often.

Family Declaration: We declare that we are full of faith for what God will do today. Every step of faith is taking us to our destiny. God's favor and blessings are chasing us down. He is faithful to meet our needs. We release our faith and receive His goodness. He is able to do exceedingly, abundantly, above and beyond all we could ask, think, or imagine. This is our declaration!

Champion: I declare I am full of faith. Every step of faith I take, God will show me what He wants me to do. I will reach my destiny. God's favor and blessings are with me. I will release my faith and receive His goodness. This is my declaration!

Family Prayer – Read the family prayer together.

Dear God,

Thank You for being with us everywhere we go. Please help us not to be afraid to do what You want us to do. Help us build our faith muscle so we can do what You want us to do. Thank You for teaching us how to be strong and courageous. Amen.

Joshua has Faith in God
Scripture Card

Deuteronomy 31:6 – Be strong and courageous. Do not be afraid because God is with you (adapted).

Joshua has Faith in God
Scripture Card

Moses was a great leader of God's people for many, many years. When he was 120 years old, he died. When Moses died, God selected a new leader for His people. The new leader's name was Joshua. God said to Joshua, "Lead my people across the Jordan River to a new land. Each place you walk on will be yours. Be strong and don't be afraid for I am with you wherever you go."

The first city God told Joshua to conquer was Jericho. Joshua was afraid because Jericho had a great wall protecting the city. Joshua's army could not go over or through the wall. Joshua asked for God's help, and God gave him a plan. Joshua decided to have faith in God and follow His plan.

God told Joshua to have his fighting men and seven priests with trumpets march around the city quietly once a day for six days. On the seventh day, they were to march around the city seven times. When they marched around the city the seventh time, the priests gave a loud blast on their trumpets and all the people of God gave a loud shout of praise to God. They watched the walls of Jericho come tumbling down. When God's people follow His plan, miracles do happen.

Even though Joshua was afraid, he had faith in God. He did what God asked him to do and good things happened. Adapted from Joshua 6:1-20.

Deuteronomy 31:6 – Be strong and courageous. Do not be afraid because God is with you (adapted).

My Faith Workout Schedule

Activity	Monday	Tuesday	Wednesday	Thursday	Friday	Saturday	Sunday
Wake up Thank God for what He is going to do today.							
Get ready for the day Read God's Word, the Bible.							
Go to School Thank God for school.							
Come home Listen to worship songs.							
Watch a positive TV show or DVD.							
Bedtime Thank God for your blessings.							

Devotional 16

Daniel Puts God First

Materials needed - 1 clear quart jar, golf ball or small ball you can write on, 4 cups of any kind of beans, bowl for the beans, and fear and comfortable faces

Scripture - Matthew 6:33 - *Put God first and He will take care of you.*

Goal - We will learn that when we are afraid, if we put God first, we can be comfortable.

I am afraid. + I put God first. = I am comfortable.

Object lesson - Tell your family about all the things that people usually do during the day. Encourage them to add to the list. While you are talking, fill a jar with the beans. Explain that the beans are the things that we do during the day. Show your family a golf ball. Write the word "God" on the ball using a black permanent marker. Tell your family, "This ball represents God's presence in our lives. Sometimes as we go through our day something happens that frightens us." Show your family the fear face. Have your family give some examples of things that frighten them. Now try to put the golf ball in the jar. Say, "We can't fit the ball in the jar because we didn't make room for God in our lives that day. We didn't put God first now when we need Him, it's hard to hear His voice."

Tell your family, "Let's try this again." Take out all of the materials and put them in a bowl, and drop the ball into the jar. Say, "The Bible says to put God first and He will take care of us. Putting God first means that we do what He wants us to do in every situation." Place the beans in the jar and say, "Now we are comfortable in any situation because God is first in our lives." Show your family the comfortable face.

Vocabulary development - Introduce the vocabulary words to the family. Talk about the meaning of each word. Acting out the meaning of the words through mime and gestures increases the understanding of the concepts.

First - most important, ahead of everything else
Fear - the belief that someone or something is likely to cause you harm
Protect - to keep safe from harm

Bible Lesson - Look at the scripture card and point out the features of the picture while you read the Bible story out loud. Read the scripture out loud and have your family members repeat it several times. Color the scripture card together. Discuss the following with your family.

- What did King Darius give Daniel? Why did he do that?
- What was the new law?
- Why didn't Daniel follow the new law?
- What happened to Daniel because he refused to follow the new law?
- How did Daniel put God first?
- How did God protect Daniel?

Application – Look at the ***Putting God First Acrostic***. Discuss the ways we can put God first each day by discussing what is on the document. Circle the first letter in each sentence. Copy the words onto the blank lines. The acrostic spells, "God First." Encourage your family to do some of the activities on the acrostic this week.

Review the scripture verse with your family often.

Family Declaration: We declare that we are putting God first in our lives. When we seek first the kingdom of God, He said He would add all of His blessings to our lives. I know He is meeting all of our needs. We don't have to worry or fear because God is in control. He is taking care of us. This is our declaration!

Champion: I declare I am putting God first in my life. When I put Him first He will add blessings to me. I know He is meeting my needs. I don't have to worry or fear because God is in control. This is my declaration!

Family Prayer – Read the family prayer together.

Dear God,

Thank You for loving us enough to take good care of us. Please teach us how to put You first each day so we can build our faith in You and be comfortable in any situation. Thank You for Your Word, the Bible, that teaches us about You. Amen.

Daniel Puts God First
Scripture Card

Matthew 6:33 - Put God first and He will take care of you (adapted).

Daniel Puts God First
Scripture Card

Daniel was a very wise man. King Darius liked him and he gave him a portion of his kingdom to rule.

There were a few people in the kingdom who were jealous of Daniel. They were Daniel's enemies. These people thought up a plan to get rid of Daniel.

They convinced King Darius to make a new law. The new law stated that everyone in the kingdom had to bow down to King Darius or be thrown into the lion's den to be eaten by the lions.

Daniel refused to bow to the king. He put God first in his life which meant he would only pray to his God.

Daniel's enemies ran to the king and told him that Daniel wasn't following his new law. The king had to follow the law, so he threw Daniel into the lion's den to spend the night with the lions. The king was very sad because he was afraid he would never see Daniel again.

Daniel was afraid, but he trusted God. He knew God would protect him because he always put God first.

In the morning, the king ran to the lion's den and shouted Daniel's name. Daniel shouted back. He said that Daniel's God had protected him. The lions did not harm Daniel. Daniel put God first, and God protected him.

King Darius was so excited that Daniel's God had protected him that he made a new law. He said everyone had to respect and bow down to Daniel's God.
Adapted from Daniel 6: 16-24.

Matthew 6:33 – Put God first and He will take care of you (adapted).

Putting God First Acrostic

Choose the best word to go in each blank space to complete the sentence. The acrostic reads, "God First."

_____ God your tithes and offerings.

_____ your parents.

_____ pray when you wake up.

_____ need to love God like I do.

_____ of sleeping in on Sundays, go to church.

_____ the Bible or listen to Bible verses.

_____ what you have with others.

_____ God for your food before you eat it.

Give
Daily
Instead
Share
Friends
Thank
Obey
Read

Devotional 17

When I am Being Bullied

Materials needed - hard bristled brush, cotton balls in a baggie, and fear and comfortable faces

Scripture - Isaiah 41:10 - *Don't be afraid, don't be discouraged. God is with you to help you and give you the victory.*

Goal - We will learn how to identify bullying behavior and how to protect ourselves when we are being bullied.

> Someone hurts me again and again.   +   I have faith that God will protect me.
> =   God can help me protect myself.

Object lesson - Have one plastic bag with cotton balls in it and a hard bristled brush available before you teach this devotional. Tell your family, "When people say and do kind things to us it makes us happy and comfortable." Show the family the comfortable face. Pass around the plastic bag with the cotton balls inside them. Allow each person to touch them. Have them describe what they feel like. An answer could be that they feel soft and good like when someone is kind to us.

Say, "When someone teases us, calls us names, bites us, kicks us, pinches us, hits us, trips us, pull our hair, and destroys our things it feels like this hard bristled brush." Pass around the brush and encourage your family to move their fingers lightly over the bristles. Say, "When people do these things to us over and over even after we have asked them to stop it is called bullying. God doesn't want us to be bullied, and he doesn't want us to act like a bully toward others. Bullies scare us." Show your family the fear face. Say, "God can help us protect ourselves from bullies so we can be comfortable again." Show your family the comfortable face.

Vocabulary development - Introduce the vocabulary words to the family. Talk about the meaning of each word. Acting out the meaning of the words through mime and gestures increases the understanding of the concepts.

Bullying - Bullying is when someone tries to make others feel uncomfortable, frightened, or sad. Bullies are people who try to control people who are smaller or younger than them.

Discouraged - when you don't want to try anymore, or you don't think that something is going to work out

Victory - being the winner in a contest or struggle

Bible Lesson - Look at the scripture card and point out the features of the picture while you read the Bible story out loud. Read the scripture out loud and have your family members repeat it several times. Color the scripture card together. Discuss the following with your family:

- What was Joseph's special gift from God?
- What did he tell his brothers?
- How did Joseph's brothers bully him? Why did they do this?
- How did Joseph's special gift help him in prison?
- Who was with Joseph through the good and the bad times?

Application - Say, "Joseph was bullied by his brothers. God used the bullying situation, that was bad, to help Joseph and others. God used Joseph to save many people from starving. God can use a bullying situation for good when we trust Him. God wants us to treat others with kindness, but He also wants us to take care of ourselves. God doesn't want us to be bullied by others.

Look at the ***What I Can Do When I Feel Bullied Card***. There are four steps we can follow to protect ourselves in a bullying situation." Read and discuss the steps with your family members. Give examples of what to do at each step. Practice the steps as a family.

Note to the family - According to research, students with disabilities are much more likely to be the target of bullying than their neuro-typical peers. Young people who experience bullying often are more likely to encounter depression, anxiety, anger, health complaints, and decreased academic achievement (Thompson, Whitney, & Smith, 1994). Therefore, it is very important that our exceptional students learn how to identify a situation where they are being bullied and protect themselves.

Review the scripture verse with your family often.

Family Declaration: We declare that no matter who comes against us, our trust is in God. God is our protector and shield in times of trouble. What can man do to us? If God is for us who can be against us? We will stay in faith in times of adversity. What was meant for our harm, God is turning around to our advantage. He is going to bring us out better than before. This is our declaration!

Champion: I declare God is my protector in times of trouble. If God is for me who can be against me? What was meant for my harm, God will turn around to my advantage. He will bring me out better than before. This is my declaration!

Family Prayer – Read the family prayer together.

Dear God,

Thank You for always being kind to us. You are a good God. Please help us to learn how to stand up to a bully. Thank You for Your protection. We know that we can do anything with You in our lives. Amen.

Joseph has Faith in God
Scripture Card

Isaiah 41:10 - Don't be afraid. Don't be discouraged. God is with you to help you and give you the victory (adapted).

Joseph has Faith in God
Scripture Card

Joseph, his father, and his 11 brothers all lived in Canaan. Joseph had a special gift. He could understand what dreams meant. Joseph's father loved him very much so he gave him a coat with many different colors. Joseph's brothers saw his coat and got very jealous.

One day Joseph had a dream and he went to tell his brothers about his dream and what it meant. He said the dream meant one day all his brothers would bow down to him. The brothers were so upset they sold Joseph into slavery. Joseph served as a slave in the home of an important man in Egypt named Potiphar.

Potiphar saw that Joseph was smart so he put him in charge of everything he owned. Things were going great for Joseph until Potiphar's wife told a lie about Joseph and her husband had Joseph put in jail. He was afraid, but God was with him.

While Joseph was in jail, he met Pharaoh's former cup bearer. A cup bearer gives Pharaoh his drinks. It is an important job. One night the cup bearer had a dream and asked Joseph to tell him what it meant. Joseph said it meant he would get out of jail and serve Pharaoh again. The dream came true.

After some time, Pharaoh had a lot of dreams he didn't understand. The cup bearer told Pharaoh about Joseph's special gift. Joseph was brought before Pharaoh and asked to tell him what his dreams meant. Joseph told Pharaoh his dream meant there would be a lot of food for seven years followed by little food for seven years.

Pharaoh believed what Joseph told him and he put Joseph in charge of all the food in Egypt. Joseph saved many people because he saved the extra food from the first seven years to feed people for the next seven years.

When there was little food left, people came from many different places to buy food from Joseph. His brothers also came, but they didn't recognize Joseph. They bowed before him and asked for food. Joseph told them who he was and that he forgave them. God turned a situation involving bullying to something good because Joseph trusted Him. Adapted from Genesis 34-45.

Isaiah 41:10 - Don't be afraid. Don't be discouraged. God is with you to help you and give you the victory (adapted).

What I Can Do When I Feel Bullied Card

Step 1:   STOP

Step 2:   WALK AWAY

Step 3:   TELL

Step 4:   PRAY to GOD

Isaiah 41:10 – Don't be afraid. Don't be discouraged. God is with you to help you and give you the victory (adapted).

Devotional 18

Helping a Friend Who is Being Bullied

Materials needed - one sheet of white computer paper, fear and comfortable faces

Scripture - Psalm 118:6 - *The Lord is for me; I will not fear; what can man do to me?*

Goal - We will learn how to help someone who is being bullied.

My friend is being bullied   +   I have faith God will protect me.
=   I can do something to help my friend.

Object lesson - Take a piece of paper and crumple it up and stomp on it. Be careful not to let the paper rip. Unfold the paper and try to smooth it out. Say, "Let's pretend the paper has feelings and the creases and dirt we see on the paper are the result of us hurting the paper's feelings. Now let's apologize to the paper for what we have done. Did the creases and dirt disappear? No, they didn't. Eventually those creases and dirt turn into scars. A scar is a mark left on the skin after it has been damaged. Sometimes bullying behavior causes scars on the inside of people. God is the only one who can heal scars.

God doesn't like bullying behavior. He doesn't want us to act like a bully and He doesn't want others to bully us. When we help others who are being bullied, God is pleased" (adapted from http: //www.buzzfeed.com/mjs538/awesome-bullying-lesson-from-a-new-york-teacher., 2013).

Vocabulary development - Introduce the vocabulary words to the family. Talk about the meaning of each word. Acting out the meaning of the words through mime and gestures increases the understanding of the concepts.

Bullying - Bullying is when someone tries to make others feel uncomfortable, frightened, or sad. Bullies are people who try to control people who are smaller or younger than them.
Fear - the feeling you have when you think you are in danger
Scar - a mark left on the skin after it has been damaged
Relatives - people in your family

Bible Lesson - Look at the scripture card and point out the features of the picture while you read the Bible story out loud. Read the scripture out loud and have your family members repeat it several times. Color the scripture card together. Discuss the following with your family:

- Who was Esther? Who were her people?
- How did the Persian people treat the Israelites?
- How did Haman act like a bully towards the Israelites?
- Who was Mordecai? What did he say to Esther?
- How did Esther help her people when they were being bullied?

Application - Show your family the fear face. Say, "God doesn't like bullying behavior. He says, 'Be kind and compassionate to one another, forgiving each other just as in Christ God forgave you.' This is found in **Ephesians 4:32.** When we bully others, we are disobeying God. God is pleased when we are kind to each other. He wants us to protect ourselves and others."

Note to the family - One important fact about bullying is that more than 50% of bullying situations stop when others get involved. Review the **Bully Buster Rules** with your family. Discuss each rule and encourage your family members to give examples of how they can follow the rules. Practice implementing the rules through the role playing scenarios generated in your discussion.

Review the scripture verse with your family often.

Family Declaration: We declare to help others as God helps us. When we defend others, we know God will be our defender. Even when we are going through challenges ourselves, the best thing we can do is be good to someone else. We will stand up for those who can't fight for themselves. We are strong, courageous, and equipped defenders for God. When the enemy surrounds us, God will protect us. God will fight for us. This is our declaration!

Champion: I declare I will help others as God helps me. When I defend others, I know God will be my defender. I will stand up for those who can't fight for themselves. I am strong, courageous, and equipped. God is fighting for us! This is my declaration!

Family Prayer – Read the family prayer together.

Dear God,

Thank You for being a mighty and strong God. You are a God who hates bullying behavior. Please teach us how to help others who are being bullied. We want to be strong and help others. Thank You for Your protection for us and the people who are important to us. Amen.

Standing up to a Bully
Scripture Card

Psalm 118:6 – The Lord is for me; I will not fear; what can man do to me?

Standing up to a Bully
Scripture Card

Xerxes, the king of Persia, married a beautiful Israelite (someone born in Israel) named Esther. She became the queen of Persia. At the time, many Israelites were slaves and being bullied by the Persian people. The king didn't know that Esther was an Israelite. Esther was an orphan. Her parents weren't alive, but she had an uncle who loved her very much named Mordecai.

Mordecai was also an Israelite like Queen Esther and he was hated by a man named Haman. Haman helped the king rule the kingdom. He was a bad man who enjoyed bullying others. Haman asked King Xerxes to make a new law which required all Israelites to be killed. Mordecai found out about the new law and told Esther that she needed to tell the king who she was before all the Israelites, including herself, would be killed.

Esther decided to stand up to the bully Haman. She had a plan. Esther prepared a great dinner for the king. This made the king very happy. At the end of dinner, the king told Esther that he wanted to do something nice for her. Esther told the king she was an Israelite. She told the king that Haman was bullying her people. The king immediately changed the law. Haman was punished. Esther saved her people and herself from a bully. Adapted from Esther 1-9:13.

Psalm 118:6 - The Lord is for me; I will not fear; what can man do to me?

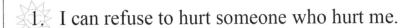

Bully Buster Rules

1. I can refuse to hurt someone who hurt me.

2. I can stand up for my friend who is being bullied.

3. I can tell an adult about what happened to my friend.

4. I can tell other kids about what happened to my friend.

5. I can refuse to repeat mean things others say about my friend.

6. I can refuse to do the mean things others do to my friend.

7. I can obey God by being a Bully Buster.

Devotional 19

Ruth Feels No Fear

Materials needed - Candle, matches or lighter, sheet of blank white paper, clear plastic or glass plate, and fear and comfortable faces

Scripture - Philippians 4:13- *I can do all things through Christ who gives me strength.*

Goal - We will learn how to do good things for others even when we are afraid to do them.

I am afraid to do something for others. + God is my strength. = I can do something for others.

Object lesson - Ask your family members to name some things they have been asked to do that frightened them. Write these things on a blank sheet of paper. Fold the paper into a fan. Light a candle. Tell your family, "This flame represents us. When I wave the fan back and forth, it creates a breeze that causes the flame to dance and possibly go out. The fan represents the things we have been asked to do that frighten us. Thinking about these things causes us to feel afraid and that fear can stop us from doing something God wants us to do. This is represented by the flame going out. Place a clear plastic or glass dish between the flame and the fan. Now have a family member wave the fan in front of the flame. Say, "Notice that the flame doesn't move when there is something in front of it to block the breeze. The clear plate represents God's love and protection. With God's love and protection, we have the strength to do anything."

Vocabulary development - Introduce the vocabulary words to the family. Talk about the meaning of each word. Acting out the meaning of the words through mime and gestures increases the understanding of the concepts.

Harvest - the season when crops are ready to be gathered from the fields

Widow- a woman whose husband is dead

Barley- a cereal grass used for breakfast foods

Famine - an extreme lack of food in a country

Bible Lesson - Look at the scripture card and point out the features of the picture while you read the Bible story out loud. Read the scripture out loud and have your family members repeat it several times. Color the scripture card together. Discuss the following with your family.

- How are Naomi, Orpah, and Ruth related?
- What happened to the women's husbands?
- After Naomi's husband and sons died, what did she decide to do?
- Why did Ruth go with her?
- What difficult thing did Naomi ask Ruth to do regarding Boaz?
- Who did Ruth marry? Who is related to Ruth and Boaz?

Application - We can do anything with Jesus' protection and strength. Talk about the pictures on the coupons. Encourage family members to choose coupons with particular tasks written on them they are afraid to do. Talk about how the tasks could be done. Break them down into steps.

Encourage family members to complete the tasks.

Review the scripture verse with your family often.

Family Declaration: We declare that God is our strength. We are filled with mountain moving faith. We are not afraid of how big or impossible a situation looks because we know God is bigger. Setbacks, strongholds, and defeat have no power over us. In faith, we say to those mountains, "Be removed because God has already given us the victory." This is our declaration!

Champion: I declare that God is my strength. I am filled with mountain moving faith. I am not afraid of how big my situation looks because I know God is bigger. Setbacks and defeat have no power over me. This is my declaration!

Family Prayer – Read the family prayer together.

Dear God,

Thank You for being our rock, our protection, and our strength. Please help us do the things You want us to do even though we are afraid to do them. Thank You for making us comfortable in any situation. Amen.

Ruth Feels No Fear
Scripture Card

Philippians 4:13 - I can do all things through Christ who gives me strength.

Ruth Feels No Fear
Scripture Card

There was a famine in the land of Bethlehem so Elimelech, his wife Naomi, and their two sons moved from Bethlehem to Moab. After a while Elimelech died but Naomi wasn't alone because she still had her two sons. Her sons married Orpah and Ruth. After several years, Naomi's sons died. The three women lived together for a period of time when Naomi decided that she wanted to return to Bethlehem. Naomi told her daughters-in-law to stay in Moab, but Ruth refused to leave her. Ruth said, "Don't ask me to leave you because where ever you go I will go, and where you stay I will stay. Your friends will be my friends and your God will be my God." Both women said good-bye to Orpah and left for Bethlehem together.

When they got to Bethlehem it was harvest time, so Ruth followed behind the harvesters in the field and picked up any barley they left behind to make a meal. Boaz was the owner of the field and he was a kind man who feared God. One day he came by to greet the harvesters and he noticed Ruth in the field gathering barley. He asked one of the harvesters who she was.

Ruth was a good woman and Naomi wanted Ruth to find a good man to marry. Naomi had a plan. She told Ruth to go to Boaz when he was asleep and cover his feet until he woke up. Ruth was afraid to do this. She had no idea what Boaz would do to her, but she obeyed Naomi.

That evening after Boaz fell asleep Ruth did what Naomi told her to do. Boaz sensing someone at his feet woke up and asked who was there. Ruth was afraid and told him that he was her kinsman redeemer. A kinsman redeemer is someone who steps into a bad situation and protects and provides for a relative. Boaz told Ruth not to be afraid because he knew she was an excellent woman and he would take care of her. Boaz married Ruth and generations later our Savior Jesus Christ was born. Adapted from the book of Ruth.

Philippians 4:13 - I can do all things through Christ who gives me strength.

Family Coupons

We can do anything with Jesus' protection and strength. Talk about the pictures on the coupons. Encourage each family member to choose one coupon with a particular task on it that they are afraid to do. Talk about how that task could be done. Break it down into steps. Practice the steps before the task is done. Praise your family members for completing the task.

This Coupon is Good for

One Hug

This Coupon is Good for

helping wash
the dirty dishes

This Coupon is Good for

making a
special treat
for someone.

This Coupon is Good for

cleaning
my room.

This Coupon is Good for

taking out
the trash.

This Coupon is Good for

spending time
with someone
doing what
he/she likes.

This Coupon is Good for

helping clean
the car.

This Coupon is Good for

helping clean
the outside
of the house.

Anxiety and Comfortable Faces

Please color, cut out, and glue the faces onto a craft stick.

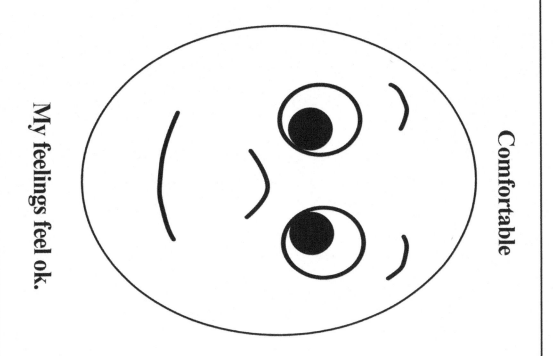

Anxiety

I feel anxious.

Comfortable

My feelings feel ok.

Devotional 20

Daniel Doesn't Worry

Materials needed - cute stuffed animal, blanket, and anxiety and comfortable faces

Scripture - Philippians 4:6 - *Do not worry about anything; instead pray about everything (adapted).*

Goal - We will learn that when we feel anxious we can ask God for help and thank Him for taking care of us.

> I feel anxious or worried.   +   I think about God.   =   I am comfortable.

Object lesson - Before the family comes into the room put a cute stuffed animal under a blanket. Don't allow anyone to look under the blanket. When everyone is seated have them guess what could be under the blanket. Talk about some of the things under the blanket that would cause us to feel anxious.

Say the following, "Anxiety is a feeling we have when we are uneasy about something or someone. It is when we are afraid something bad will happen, but it hasn't happened yet. When we are anxious, we can look like this." Show them the anxiety face. Model what being anxious looks like with your body by clenching your jaw, bulging your eyes, and wringing your hands.

Lift up the blanket and let everyone see what is under the blanket. Let them know that there was nothing to be anxious about. God doesn't want us to be anxious about anything, but instead trust Him in all things.

Vocabulary development - Introduce the vocabulary words to the family. Talk about the meaning of each word. Acting out the meaning of the words through mime and gestures increases the understanding of the concepts.

> **Anxiety** - upset or worried about something that hasn't happened or may not happen
> **Thoughts** - ideas
> **Feeling** - emotions
> **Action** - what you do

Bible Lesson - Look at the scripture card and point out the features of the picture while you read the Bible story out loud. Read the scripture out loud and have your family members repeat it several times. Color the scripture card together. Discuss the following with your family.

- What did Nebuchadnezzar do to the Israelites (God's people)?
- What did Nebuchadnezzar require Daniel and the other young men to do while they were in the palace?
- What did Daniel do instead of following Nebuchadnezzar's rules?
- Do you think Daniel was anxious about his decision?
- What happened when Daniel obeyed God instead of Nebuchadnezzar?
- What did the king decide to do after he heard about Daniel's diet?

Application - Review the following equation. Say, "What we think affects how we feel and how we feel influences how we act." Review the diagram with your family.

Our Thoughts ➔ Our Feelings ➔ Our Actions

Say, "There are many things that may cause us to feel anxious. Some of these things could include going to a new place, hearing strange noises at night, not liking the food we are told to eat, or going to the dentist or the doctor." Encourage your family members to share with each other something that makes them anxious.

Continue with, "When we are anxious our bodies can feel a certain way." Point to the parts on your body as you say the following, "Our heart beats faster, we breathe faster than we normally would, we sweat a lot, our muscles are tight, sometimes we cry, our bodies shake, and we feel like we want to scream."

Say, "Anxiety feels like fear, but it is a false alarm. Anxiety can sometimes keep us from doing good things. We can change the ways our bodies feel when we change what we are thinking. When we are anxious, we can remember the following:

• We can think about how much God loves us and that He will never leave us.
• Read or listen to God's Word, the Bible, over and over until you feel comfortable.
• Pray to God for help. We can say, 'God please help us feel comfortable.'
• Praise God for all the good things in our lives.
• Talk to an adult or friend about how we are feeling.
• Do something we like to do.
• Listen to worship music.
• Manipulate a fidget toy."

Review the scripture verse with your family often.

Family Declaration: We declare that we are letting go of worry. Every day we will say, "Nothing is impossible with God." There is no obstacle too difficult to overcome. God has equipped us with everything we need to accomplish what we could never do on our own. We are overcomers through the power of God. This is our declaration!

Champion: I declare I'm not going worry. When I feel anxious I will think about God and He will make me comfortable. He will help me reach my goals. I will put my trust in God. I am an overcomer. This is my declaration!

Family Prayer – Read the family prayer together.

Dear God,

Thank You for being a wonderful God. Please help us feel comfortable in situations where we feel anxious. Please help us keep our thoughts on all the blessings You have given us. Thank You for loving us and wanting the best for us. Amen.

Daniel Doesn't Worry
Scripture Card

Philippians 4:6 - Do not worry about anything; instead pray about everything (adapted).

Daniel Doesn't Worry
Scripture Card

King Nebuchadnezzar conquered the city where God's people, the Israelites, lived. He made all the Israelites his slaves. He took the smartest and strongest Israelite young men away from their families and made them live in the palace with him. Daniel was one of these young men.

Daniel loved God and followed His Commandments. While Daniel was at the palace, he had to do what the king wanted. The king wanted Daniel to eat the food he gave him. The king's food was good food, but it wasn't the food God wanted Daniel to eat. Daniel had to make a choice. He decided to do what God wanted him to do. The person in charge of giving Daniel his food each day got very anxious about Daniel not eating the king's food. He knew that the king would punish him if Daniel didn't look as good as the other boys who ate the king's food. Daniel trusted God and wasn't anxious about what could happen. Daniel told the man not to be anxious because his God could be trusted. Daniel told the man he would go off God's diet if after ten days of being on it he wasn't as healthy as the other boys. The man agreed, but he was still very anxious.

Ten days later, the king was watching Daniel and the other boys run. He noticed Daniel ran faster and looked healthier than the other boys. The king spoke to the man in charge of Daniel and the other boys' diet. The king said, "What special foods are you giving to Daniel that you are not giving to the other boys?" The man answered the king truthfully. He told the king about his deal with Daniel. Immediately upon hearing this, the king ordered all the boys to have the same diet as Daniel.

God's Word tells us not to worry about anything, but instead to trust Him to give us what we need when we do what He asks. Adapted from Daniel 1:1-20.

Philippians 4:6 - Do not worry about anything; instead pray about everything (adapted).

Devotional 21

Noah Doesn't Worry About the Future

Materials needed - your family albums, family pictures of major events, anxiety and comfortable faces

Scripture - Jeremiah 7:23-24 - *Obey me, and I will be your God and you will be my child. Do what I command you and everything will be ok (adapted).*

Goal - We will understand that even when we are anxious about the future, if we obey God everything will be ok.

> I am anxious about the future.   +   I obey God anyway.   =   I am comfortable.

Object lesson - Look at some family albums. Talk about major life events. Be sure to discuss a time when you were anxious about doing something God wanted you to do, but you chose to obey God and everything turned out ok. God's Word says, "Obey me, and I will be your God and you will be my child. Do what I command you and everything will be ok." (adapted Jeremiah 7:23-24).

Vocabulary development - Introduce the vocabulary words to the family. Talk about the meaning of each word. Acting out the meaning of the words through mime and gestures increases the understanding of the concepts.

> **Obey** - to listen and do what God says
> **Command** - when God tells us to do something
> **Well** - things are OK

Bible Lesson - Look at the scripture card and point out the features of the picture while you read the Bible story out loud. Read the scripture out loud and have your family members repeat it several times. Color the scripture card together. Discuss the following with your family.

- What did God tell Noah to do?
- Did Noah obey God?
- Do you think Noah was anxious about doing what God wanted him to do?
- After Noah finished the ark, what did God ask him to do?
- How many days did it rain?
- What did Noah do when he stepped off the ark?

Application - Tell your family, "We know when we obey God, we don't need to be anxious about the future because He will take care of us. He wants the best for us." Have your family look at the *Obeying God Journal*. Explain that a journal is a blank book where you write about the major events in your life. It's a place where you write your thoughts and ideas. Discuss the activities on the page. The activities are pray before meals, share my things with others, and obey my parents. Encourage your family members to do these activities daily. Place a check mark next to each item as you complete it each day. Feel free to add to the journal. If you laminate the page, it can be reused.

Review the scripture verse with your family often.

Family Declaration: We declare we will not worry about the future. We will obey God and trust Him. We will look for new opportunities God has for us. We choose not to settle, but to grab hold of the dreams God has put in our hearts. This is our declaration!

Champion: I declare I will not worry about the future. I will obey and trust God because He is taking care of me. I will dream big and pursue my God-given dreams. This is my declaration!

Family Prayer – Read the family prayer together.

Dear God,

Thank You for giving us a future with You. Sometimes we are anxious about what will happen tomorrow. Please help us to remember that all we have to do is obey You and everything will be OK. Thank You for the plan You have made for us. Thank You for the good things that are coming our way. Amen.

Noah Doesn't Worry About the Future
Scripture Card

Jeremiah 7:23-24 - Obey me, and I will be your God and you will be My child. Do what I command you and everything will be OK (adapted).

Noah Doesn't Worry About the Future
Scripture Card

When Noah lived on the Earth, he and his family were the only people who followed God's commandments. God was very upset about this. God told Noah to build a large boat, or ark, because God was going to make it rain until all the Earth was flooded and there was nothing left alive. God told Noah how to build the ark. If Noah and his family were in the ark when the rains came, they would be safe.

Noah began building the ark. Noah didn't know when it would rain, or if the ark would float. There were times when he was anxious and worried about the future, but he obeyed God anyway.

Shortly before the rain began, God told Noah to bring his family and two of every kind of creature, male and female, into the ark. As soon as all the creatures and Noah's family were in the ark, it began to rain. It rained for 40 days and nights. The whole earth was flooded and everything died that wasn't in the ark.

Many days after God made the rain stop, Noah, his family, and all the living creatures in the ark stepped out of the ark onto dry land. When Noah came out of the ark, he was so thankful God saved his family that he took time to honor God and thank Him for giving him a future. God was very pleased with Noah and promised never to flood the earth again. God made the rainbow to remind us of His promises. Adapted from Genesis chapters 6, 7, 8, 9:1.

Jeremiah 7:23-24 - Obey me, and I will be your God and you will be My child. Do what I command you and everything will be OK (adapted).

Obeying God Journal

I am anxious about obeying God.   +   I obey God anyway.   =   I am comfortable.

Jeremiah 7:23-24 - *Obey me, and I will be your God and you will be My child. Do what I command you and everything will be OK (adapted).*

Put a check mark next to the ways you choose to obey God today.

_____Pray before meals.

_____Share my things with others.

_____Obey my parents.

How I feel when I obey God:_____

Devotional 22

I Can Try New Things

Materials needed - wig or something unusual to wear, and anxiety and comfortable faces

Scripture - John 10:10 - *Jesus came to give us a life filled with good things (adapted).*

Goal - We will learn how to control our anxiety by trusting God to help us do new things.

I am anxious about trying new things. +   God is with me. =   I can try new things.

Object lesson - Come into the room wearing a wig or something very different than you usually wear. Say the following to the family, "Does anyone notice something different about me today?" Wait for a response. Continue with, "Yes, I am wearing a wig. I was anxious about wearing the wig today because I wasn't sure how it would fit, how it would feel, or what people would say to me. Here is how I felt when I first put the wig on." Show your family the anxious feeling face and tell them you felt anxious. Say, "I was a little anxious at first about wearing the wig, but after a while I liked wearing it. I like wearing something new. I now feel comfortable about wearing this wig." Show your family the comfortable feeling face.

Say, "God has made the world big, beautiful, and full of great things. There is so much to experience and do. God wants us to enjoy life and try new things. His Word says, *Jesus came to give us a life filled with good things"* (John 10:10 adapted).

Vocabulary development - Introduce the vocabulary words to the family. Talk about the meaning of each word. Acting out the meaning of the words through mime and gestures increases the understanding of the concepts.

> **Full** - holding as much as possible, no empty space
> **Pharaoh** - ruler of Egypt
> **Stutter** - a difficulty with moving from one sound to the next when speaking, or a difficulty
> with starting or stopping speech

Bible Lesson - Look at the scripture card and point out the features of the picture while you read the Bible story out loud. Read the scripture out loud and have your family members repeat it several times. Color the scripture card together. Discuss the following with your family.

- Who wanted to kill Moses and all the young Hebrew boys?
- What did Moses' mother do to save his life?
- Who found Moses in the water and adopted him?
- Why did Moses leave the palace?
- How did God use the changes in Moses' life to save His people?

Moses was one of the most powerful men in the Bible. Moses had to trust God as he experienced a lot of new and different things in his life.

Application - Say, "God made a lot of wonderful things in this world. This week let's agree to try something new. We can try a new game, or go to a new place, or try a new look, or try a new food. Let's complete the *I am Trying Something New chart* together."

Have the family members talk about a time when they felt anxious and how thinking about God being with them helped them feel comfortable again.

Review the scripture verse with your family often.

Family Declaration: We declare we are going to try new things. We will not let circumstances stop us from living a full life. We are crowned with God's favor. His plans for us will take us further than we ever imagined. As we step out into new adventures, we know God is going to prosper us. We are excited about the blessings He's sending our way. We accept the fullness of what God has in store for us. This is our declaration!

Champion: I declare I will try new things. I will not let anything stop me from living the life God has planned for me. As I try new things, God will protect me and keep me safe. I am excited about the new adventures God and I will have together. This is my declaration!

Family Prayer – Read the family prayer together.

Dear God,

Thank You for filling this world with wonderful things. Please help us try new things. We know we can do new things with Your help. Thank You for being an awesome God. Amen.

Moses Does Something New
Scripture Card

John 10:10 - Jesus came to give us a life filled with good things (adapted).

Moses Does Something New
Scripture Card

Moses was one of the most powerful men in the Bible. Moses had to trust God as he experienced a lot of new and different things in his life.

Moses was born a Hebrew slave. His family was very poor and worked hard for Pharaoh, the king of Egypt. When Moses was a baby, Pharaoh decided to have all the young Hebrew boys killed. Moses' mother put him in a basket and placed him into the river so Pharaoh's soldiers couldn't find him and kill him. Pharaoh's daughter was near the water when she saw the basket and took it out of the water. She saw Moses and decided to keep him and raise him like he was her own son. For the next several years, Moses lived in the palace in Egypt as a prince.

Moses lived in the palace until he was a young man. One day he saw an Egyptian beating a Hebrew slave. He lost his temper and killed the Egyptian. Moses ran away into the wilderness because if Pharaoh found out what Moses did, he would kill him. Living in the wilderness was a big change for Moses.

Moses became a shepherd. He took care of sheep. One day Moses was watching the sheep and he noticed a burning bush that never stopped burning. This was very unusual. God's voice came from the bush. God told Moses to remove his sandals because where he stood was holy ground. God told Moses to go back to Egypt and tell the Pharaoh to free the Hebrew slaves.

Moses didn't want to go back to Egypt because he thought Pharaoh would remember that he had killed an Egyptian. The penalty for killing someone was death. Moses didn't want to speak to Pharaoh because he stuttered and this embarrassed him. Moses remembered that God helped him through every new and different experience. Even though Moses was anxious, he did what God wanted him to do. He obeyed God and God used him to free God's people from their slavery in Egypt. Adapted from Exodus chapters 1-14.

John 10:10 - Jesus came to give us a life filled with good things (adapted).

I Am Trying Something New

Complete the chart together by writing the name of each individual in the first column. Write or draw a picture of something new each individual will do in the second column. After the task is complete, write or draw a picture of how it felt to try something new in the third column.

Name	Something new	How I felt

Devotional 23

Inviting a Friend to Church

Materials needed - 64 small pieces of candy, or stickers, or small erasers, or unsharpened pencils, a brown paper bag, and anxious and comfortable faces

Scripture - Mark 16: 15 - *Jesus said, "Go into all the world and preach the gospel" (adapted).*

Goal - We will learn how to overcome our anxiety about inviting others to church and talking to them about God's love.

I am anxious about telling others about Jesus.   +   I can invite someone to church.
=   God is pleased.

Object lesson - Before the devotional, place 64 small objects like stickers, individually wrapped pieces of candy, or pencils in a paper bag. Take out one object and say, "This object represents the first person to ever come to church and accept Jesus as his/her personal Savior." Bring out another object and explain to your family, "The first person asked a friend to come to church. The friend came to church and asked Jesus to become his/her personal Savior. Now there were two people who were Christ followers." Show your family the two objects. Say, "Those two people each invited a friend to church. These people came to church and asked Jesus to be their personal Savior. Now there were four people who were Christ followers." Show your family the four objects. Say, "Soon those four students each asked someone to come to church with them. These people came to church and asked Jesus to be their personal Savior. Now there were eight Christ followers." Continue the pattern to sixteen. At sixteen, dump the remainder of the objects out onto the table. Continue with, "When each of us tells others about Jesus and asks them to come to church, many people will have the opportunity to accept Jesus as their personal Savior. This pleases God."
(adapted from http://www.ehow.com/info_8306660_sunday-school-object-lessons-fiveyearolds.html, 2013).

Vocabulary development - Introduce the vocabulary words to the family. Talk about the meaning of each word. Acting out the meaning of the words through mime and gestures increases the understanding of the concepts.

    Gospel - the good news that Jesus came to save us from our sins so we could be in His family forever
    Invite - to ask someone to do something with you

Bible Lesson - Look at the scripture card and point out the features of the picture while you read the Bible story out loud. Read the scripture out loud and have your family members repeat it several times. Color the scripture card together. Discuss the following with your family.

- Why did Jesus come to the Earth?
- What do we have to do to be saved or be part of God's family forever?
- What does God want us to do once we are saved?
- What are the three things we can tell others about Jesus?
- Why is it important to share the Gospel with others?

Application - Read, discuss, and model the steps on the *Inviting a Friend to Church Conversation Cards.* Practice inviting others to church using the *Inviting a Friend to Church Conversation Cards* for visual support. Invite a friend to church this week..

Note to families -Use a hula hoop to teach your family members about personal space. Personal space is the physical space surrounding a person. Invading someone's personal space may cause him/her to feel uncomfortable or anxious. When you practice inviting someone to church or have any conversation, have one person stand in the hula hoop and another person stand outside the hula hoop. The space inside the hula hoop represents the person's personal space. Encourage family members to respect the personal space of others.

Review the scripture verse with your family often.

Family Declaration: We declare we will be a witness to others. People need what we can give. We will not be afraid to share about God's goodness. God is giving us influence that will cause others to want to be around us. We will share the good news and shine His light wherever we go. God will use us to be world shakers and history makers. This is our declaration!

Champion: I declare I will talk to others about God. People need what I have to give. I will not be afraid to share what God has done for me (my testimony). God is helping me talk about His love to my friends. He will use me to be a world shaker and history maker. This is my declaration!

Family Prayer – Read the family prayer together.

Dear God,

Thank You for sending Jesus to us to save us from our sins. Please help us share this good news with others. Thank You for allowing me to be part of Your family. Amen.

Jesus, my Lord and Savior!
Scripture Card

He listens to me.

He is my Savior.

He loves me.

Mark 16:15 - Jesus said, "Go into all the world and preach the gospel" (adapted).

Jesus, my Lord and Savior!
Scripture Card

We know that God sent Jesus to the Earth to teach us how to live the right way, and to die on the cross for our sins. When we believe Jesus is God's Son and ask God to forgive our sins, or the things we have done wrong, we are saved. After Jesus died on the cross, He came back to life. Before He left the earth to go back to Heaven, He commanded His disciples to "Go into all the world and preach the gospel to all creation." If we are Christians we are disciples of Jesus so we need to obey His Commandments. Jesus wants us to go and tell others about Him.

Sharing the good news about Jesus is like sharing a fabulous gift with someone. Jesus is the best thing in our lives. He saved us from our sins so we can live with Him forever in Heaven when we die. It is important that we tell our family and friends about the amazing gift of Jesus. We can tell our family and friends the following. We can tell others that Jesus listens to us, He is our Savior, and He loves us.

Tell everyone about what Jesus is like. He is a good listener. Jesus listens to us when we pray or talk to Him. He answers prayer. **Jeremiah 29:12** - *Then you will call on me and come and pray to me, and I will listen to you.*

Tell everyone that Jesus is our Savior. He saves us and protects us from harm. He saves us so we can be in His family forever. To be in God's family forever, we must believe that Jesus is the Son of God and that He died on the cross for our sins. If we ask Him to forgive us for not following His commandments, He will forgive us and we can live with Him forever. God's Word says, **John 3:16** - *For God so loved the world that He gave His one and only son, that whoever believes in Him shall not perish but have eternal life.*

Tell everyone that Jesus loves us. God's Word says, **Psalm 103:11** - *For as high as the heavens are above the Earth, so great is his love for those who fear him.* Adapted from Matthew 28:16-20.

Mark 16:15 - Jesus said, "Go into all the world and preach the gospel" (adapted).

Inviting a Friend to Church Conversation Cards

Use the *Inviting a Friend to Church Conversation Cards* as you model how to invite a friend to church. Read each card while showing your family members what to do. Have the family members reverse roles. This gives each member of the family the opportunity to see things from another person's perspective. Understanding another person's point of view is essential in the development of social skills.

1 Begin a conversation. Say, "Hi!" Wait for the person to respond.
He says, "Hi."

CONVERSATION CARDS
Inviting a Friend to Church

2 Say, "Would you like to go to Church with me?"

Wait for the person to respond.

CONVERSATION CARDS
Inviting a Friend to Church

3 Your friend says, "Yes." Say, "Here is my phone number. Have your mom call my mom so we can get together."

If your friend says, "No," then say, "Maybe next time."

CONVERSATION CARDS
Inviting a Friend to Church

church

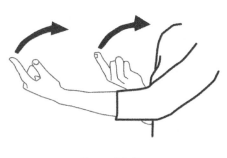

come

Devotional 24

Public and Private Behavior

Materials needed – tooth brush, and anxious and comfortable faces

Scripture - Romans 12:18 - *Do all that you can to live at peace with everyone.*

Goal - We will learn about the difference between public and private places and public and private behaviors. We will learn that when we do private behaviors in public we cause others to feel anxious and uncomfortable. God wants us to live at peace with everyone.

> There are public and private behaviors.   +   I keep my private behaviors private.
> =   The people around me aren't anxious, and God is pleased.

Object lesson - As you begin the devotional, put a tooth brush in your mouth and rigorously brush your teeth. Say, "God wants us all to live at peace with everyone. He wants us to be the kind of person that people feel comfortable to be around. One way we can do this is to keep our private behaviors private. Private behaviors are those things we do when we are alone or sometimes with our parent. Some examples of these behaviors are using the restroom, changing our clothes, taking a bath, or brushing our teeth." Stop talking, and take the toothbrush out of your mouth. Then say, "Oops, I am brushing my teeth in front of everyone in the family. I am doing a private behavior in public. When we do private behaviors in public, it can cause people around us to feel anxious and uncomfortable. When people feel uncomfortable and anxious, they often don't want to be around us."

Vocabulary development - Introduce the vocabulary words to the family. Talk about the meaning of each word. Acting out the meaning of the words through mime and gestures increases the understanding of the concepts.

> **Private behavior -** things we do when we are alone
> **Public behavior -** things we do when we are with others
> **Peace -** comfortable, calm, quiet

Bible Lesson - Look at the scripture card and point out the features of the picture while you read the Bible story out loud. Read the scripture out loud and have your family members repeat it several times. Color the scripture card together. Discuss the following with your family.

- Who was David?
- What was he doing on the balcony?
- What was Bathsheba doing?
- Why was it wrong for David to look at Bathsheba?
- How did God feel about David's behavior?

Application - Say, "There are two types of places and two kinds of behavior. God wants us to live at peace with everyone. Living at peace with others means we don't do things that cause them to be uncomfortable and anxious around us. To do this we must keep our private behaviors private. We make others comfortable by doing private behaviors only in private places."

Say, "There are two types of places; public and private. Public places are those places shared by many. Some examples of these places are: school, church, stores, and the park. Private places are places where we are alone or with our parents. Private places include: your home, your bedroom, the bathroom, or behind a closed door. Just like there are public and private places, there are public and private behaviors.

Public behaviors are those behaviors we do with others around us." Read the public behaviors out loud and have your family act them out.

- Eating
- Swimming with your bathing suit on
- Walking, jogging, running
- Talking to others
- Swinging on a swing
- Rocking in a rocking chair
- Listening to music
- Holding a fidget toy

Continue with: "Private behaviors are those behaviors we do alone or with our parents." Read the list of private behaviors out loud to your family. Discuss why you may not want to do these behaviors in public.

- Brushing your teeth
- Using the restroom
- Taking off your clothes
- Picking your nose
- Excessive rocking
- Excessive hand flapping or other repetitive behaviors
- Burping loudly
- Licking things that aren't food
- Farting (passing gas)

Say, "We can help each other stop doing a private behavior in public. When you see a family member doing a private behavior in public, give them a hand signal. The hand signal is the sign language letter 'P' for private." As a family, you can use this signal or establish a different one. Remind everyone to be very careful about not hurting someone's feelings when you see them doing a private behavior in public. Tell them, "Don't draw attention to someone doing a private behavior in public, but respectfully show them the signal. We don't want to embarrass our family members."

Review the scripture verse with your family often.

Family Declaration: We declare that we will be peacemakers through our actions. We will be an example that people want to be around. We are going to live a life of excellence and integrity. We will not sow seeds of negative behavior at any time or anywhere. By faith God is helping us break every bad habit, public or private, so we can honor Him with our lives. We will let our lives shine before people and impact future generations. This is our declaration!

Champion: I declare I will be a peacemaker through my actions. I will be an example of how to live peacefully with my family and friends. I am going to live a life that pleases God. By faith God is helping me break every bad habit, public or private, so I can live a life that honors Him. I will let my life shine. This is my declaration!

Family Prayer – Read the family prayer together.

Dear God,

Thank You for being our best friend. We know that You want us to be a friend to others. We know that to make friends with others they need to feel comfortable being around us. To make sure they are comfortable, we need to keep our private behaviors private. Please help us do that. Thank You for always wanting to be around us no manner how we are acting. Amen.

When Private Things Become Public
Scripture Card

Romans 12:18 - Do all that you can to live at peace with everyone.

When Private Things Become Public
Scripture Card

Israel had a great king named David. David had a large family, and lived in a huge, wonderful palace. David's army was currently fighting the Ammonites. David chose not to fight this battle with his army, but instead he stayed at home with his family. He was happy and was enjoying God's blessings in his life.

One evening he went out onto the balcony of the palace that looked out over the city. As he was on his balcony, he noticed a woman getting ready to take a bath. She was very beautiful. He found out later that her name was Bathsheba. Taking a bath is private behavior, and it is something we do during our private time. David knew taking a bath was private behavior done during someone's private time. He knew he wasn't suppose to look at Bathsheba while she bathed, but he chose to look at her anyway.

His behavior displeased God and caused David to sin. God wants us to live at peace with all people. We can do this by respecting others' private time. Adapted from 2 Samuel 12: 1-18.

Romans 12:18 – Do all that you can to live at peace with everyone.

Devotional 25

Solomon Prays for Wisdom

Materials needed – tooth brush, a favorite sweet, and anxious and comfortable faces.

Scripture - James 1: 5 - *If you believe you need wisdom, ask God for it and He will give it to you freely (adapted).*

Goal - We will learn that we can ask God for wisdom when we don't know what to do and He will give it to us.

I am anxious about doing something I don't know how to do. + I ask God for help.
= God helps me, and I am comfortable.

Object lesson - Have a favorite treat available for the family to see. Don't share it with your family members yet. Say the following, "Have you ever wanted what others had? What is the best way to get something you want?" Wait for your family members to answer your questions. Make sure that you discuss that the best way to get what you want is to ask for it using polite words like "Please" and "Thank you". Continue with, "When you received what you wanted how did it feel?" Show your family the feeling faces to help them identify their feelings.

Say, "God wants us to have a great life. In order to do that, we must have wisdom. Wisdom is knowing what the right thing to do is and doing it. God says all we have to do is ask Him for wisdom and He will give it to us. Asking for wisdom is as easy as asking for one of the treats I have." Encourage your family members to ask for a treat using polite words and share the treats with them.

Vocabulary development - Introduce the vocabulary words to the family. Talk about the meaning of each word. Acting out the meaning of the words through mime and gestures increases the understanding of the concepts.

Wisdom - the ability to understand things- It is knowing what the right thing to do is.
Anxiety - upset or worried about something that hasn't happened or may not happen

Bible Lesson - Look at the scripture card and point out the features of the picture while you read the Bible story out loud. Read the scripture out loud and have your family members repeat it several times. Color the scripture card together. Discuss the following with your family.

- Who was Solomon's father?
- Why was Solomon anxious?
- What did Solomon ask God for?
- What did God promise to give Solomon as long as he followed God's commandments?

Application - Say, "If wisdom is very important to have, where do we obtain wisdom? Proverbs 2:6 says, *"For the Lord gives wisdom, and from his mouth come knowledge and understanding."* There are several ways to get wisdom, here are a few:

- All wisdom comes from God. The Bible is the Word of God; therefore reading and hearing God's Word gives us wisdom.
- Talk to people who love and obey God.

- Watch what people who love and obey God do, and do the same thing.
- Listen to people who love and obey God. Do what they ask you to do."

Review the scripture verse with your family often.

Family Declaration: We declare we are growing in God's wisdom. We are open to the plans God has for our lives. His ways are so much higher. Even when we don't understand why something may happen the way it does, we know God's ways are better than ours. When God does something different than we expect, we will be willing to try it His way so we can experience His best. This is our declaration!

Champion: I declare I am growing in God's wisdom. I will be open to the plans God has for my life. His ways are so much higher than mine. Even when I don't understand, I will trust that He knows what is best for my life. This is my declaration!

Family Prayer – Read the family prayer together.

Dear God,

Thank You for giving us wisdom when we ask for it. Please help us make wise choices every day. Thank You for loving us enough to send Jesus who taught us how to be wise. Amen.

Solomon Prays for Wisdom
Scripture Card

James 1: 5 – If you believe you need wisdom, ask God for it and He will give it to you freely (adapted).

Solomon Prays for Wisdom
Scripture Card

David loved God and tried to live a life that pleased Him. When King David died, his son Solomon became king. Solomon was very young when he became king and was anxious about ruling God's people. One night God came to Solomon while he was dreaming and said, "Because your father David pleased me so much, ask me for whatever you want and I will give it to you."

Solomon answered, "You are a great God. You have been wonderful to my father, David, now You have made me king. I feel anxious because I am young and I can't rule Your people without wisdom. Please give me the wisdom to rule Your people well. Please help me know the difference between right and wrong and give me the strength to always do the right thing."

God was so pleased that Solomon asked for wisdom, He did something truly wonderful for Solomon. God said to Solomon, "Since you have asked for wisdom and not for a long life or a lot of money, I will give you what you asked for and much more. If you keep My commandments as your father David did, I will give you wisdom, a long life, and great wealth." God kept His promise to Solomon and Solomon became very famous because of his wisdom and great wealth. Adapted from 1 Kings 3:1-28.

James 1: 5 – If you believe you need wisdom, ask God for it and He will give it to you freely (adapted).

Angry and Comfortable Faces

Please color, cut out, and glue the faces onto a craft stick.

Angry

I feel angry.

Comfortable

My feelings feel ok.

Devotional 26

What do I do When I am Angry?

Materials needed – balloon, and anger and comfortable faces

Scripture - Ephesians 4: 32 - *Be kind to one another, forgiving each other, just as God forgave you (adapted).*

Goal - We will learn that God can help us control our anger so that when we are angry we don't hurt anyone.

I feel angry. + I think about God. = I am comfortable.

Object lesson - Hold up a balloon and say, "This balloon holds anger. The air that I blow into the balloon represents anger. The following things sometimes make us angry." (After each sentence is said blow a breath of air into the balloon. Hold the top of the balloon closed so the air doesn't escape). Say the following out loud,

- "Someone took something of ours without asking.
- Someone hits us.
- Someone calls us names.
- Someone refuses to share with us."

Say, "When we are angry, sometimes it is hard to stop being angry. Sometimes we get so angry we feel like we are going to pop just like the balloon. When we pop we have to be careful not to hurt others. Being angry is ok with God, but hurting others when we are angry is not ok. The best way to control our anger is to ask for God's help. Asking for God's help is like releasing the air in this balloon slowly." Slowly release the air in the balloon by carefully relaxing your grip on the end of the balloon.

Vocabulary development - Introduce the vocabulary words to the family. Talk about the meaning of each word. Acting out the meaning of the words through mime and gesture increases the understanding of the concepts.

> **Anger -** a strong feeling of being upset or frustrated; an overwhelming feeling of fear or hurt.
> **Forgive -** stop being angry at someone who has hurt you

Bible Lesson - Look at the scripture card and point out the features of the picture while you read the Bible story out loud. Read the scripture out loud and have your family members repeat it several times. Color the scripture card together. Discuss the following with your family.

- What did the younger son want from his father?
- Why did the younger son get a job feeding pigs?
- What did the father do when he saw his younger son come home?
- How did the older brother feel about his brother coming home after he had spent all the money their father gave him?
- What does God want us to do when we are angry?

Say, "There are many things that make us angry." Show the family the anger face. Encourage family members to share situations that cause them to feel anger. Point to the body parts as you say the following, "When we are angry, our bodies feel a certain way. Sometimes our bodies shake, our face gets hot and sweaty, our stomach aches, we feel like hitting someone, we want to scream, our heart beats very fast, we breathe faster than we normally do, and our muscles are tight and tense.

We can change our feelings of anger into comfort when we remember how much God loves us. We can think about how He forgives us for the things we do wrong when we ask Him to. God wants us to forgive others just like He forgives us. If we truly forgive others for something they have done wrong, we can let go of our anger and feel comfortable again." Show the family the comfortable face. Continue with, "Some other things we can do to help us feel comfortable are as follows:

- Pray to God for help. We can say, 'God please help me feel comfortable again.'
- Before we do or say anything, count down from ten to one slowly.
- Thank God for all the great things He has given you.
- Talk to an adult or friend about how you are feeling.
- Do something you like to do.
- Listen to worship music.
- Write a note to the person who hurt you.
- Squeeze or play with a fidget toy.

Review the scripture verse with your family often.

Family Declaration: We declare that we will not let anger control our thoughts. We will pause, let it go, and give it to God. When we feel anger, we will not hurt others. God is replacing our anger with feelings of love, hope, and peace. No matter how angry we feel, we proclaim that God is in control and we can trust Him. This is our declaration!

Champion: I declare I will not let anger control my thoughts. I will stop thinking about the things that make me angry. I will let God know how I feel and why, then let the angry feelings go. When I feel angry, I will not hurt others. God is replacing my anger with feelings of love, hope, and peace. This is my declaration!

Family Prayer – Read the family prayer together.

Dear God,

Thank You for forgiving us every time we ask You to. Please help us forgive people who hurt us just like You forgive us when we don't follow Your Commandments. Thank You for loving us. We love You. Amen.

What do I do When I am Angry
Scripture Card

Ephesians 4:32 - *Be kind to one another, forgiving each other, just as God forgave you (adapted).*

What do I do When I am Angry
Scripture Card

There once was a father who had two sons. This family lived on a large farm. The younger son was tired of working on the farm so he asked his father for all the money he had saved for him. The father gave it to him and the son left his home.

Soon the son spent all the money. He had nothing left, so he took a job feeding pigs. This job didn't pay him enough to buy the food he needed so he was hungry. He decided to go back home and ask his father to forgive him for the bad choices he made. He would ask his father to give him a job so he could buy food.

When the father saw his son walking home, he was so excited. He ran to his son, threw his arms around him and kissed him. Then, his father gave him a big party.

The older son saw what was happening and was angry. He had always worked hard for the father and never asked for extra money. The father saw how angry his older son was. He told his older son to appreciate having all the things the father gave him and to forgive his brother.

God wants us to have the same attitude towards each other as the father in the story, not the older brother. When others hurt us, and we become angry, God wants us to forgive them just like He forgives us. Adapted from Luke 15:11-32.

Ephesians 4:32 - *Be kind to one another, forgiving each other, just as God forgave you (adapted).*

Devotional 27

Why Should I Forgive?

Materials needed – small inexpensive gifts like stickers, individually wrapped candies, pencils, and angry and comfortable faces

Scripture - Luke 11:4 - *God forgives me, so I forgive everyone who has hurt me (adapted).*

Goal - We will learn that it is important to forgive others when they hurt us. When we forgive others it's like giving them a gift.

Someone hurt me and I am angry.   +   God forgives me when I ask Him.
+   I will forgive the person who hurt me.   =   I am comfortable.

Object lesson - Give each family member a small gift like a sticker, sweet treat, or pencil, or a favorite piece of candy. Encourage everyone receiving a gift to say or sign "thank you" when they receive the gift. Say, "God gave us a wonderful gift and that was Jesus. Jesus died for our sins. When we ask for forgiveness when we have done something wrong, God forgives us because of what Jesus did. Forgiveness is a gift God gives to us. It is a gift God wants us to give others. Forgiving others is a gift we give to the people who hurt us. It also helps us feel comfortable again and this pleases God."

Vocabulary development - Introduce the vocabulary words to the family. Talk about the meaning of each word. Acting out the meaning of the words through mime and gestures increases the understanding of the concepts.

Merciful - compassion, forgiveness
Forgive - stop feeling angry towards something or someone who has hurt you
Hurt - to cause physical or emotional pain
Anger - A strong feeling of being upset and frustrated; an overwhelming feeling of fear or hurt

Bible Lesson - Look at the scripture card and point out the features of the picture while you read the Bible story out loud. Read the scripture out loud and have your family members repeat it several times. Color the scripture card together. Discuss the following with your family.

- What did the servant ask the king to do?
- What did the king do?
- What did the servant do after the king forgave him?
- What did the king do when he found out the servant he forgave didn't forgive the person who owed him money?

Application - Show your family the Tree People. Say, "The Tree People look like people from the waist up and trees with trunks and roots from the waist down. Tree People travel by moving their roots from side to side. As they travel, they pick up trash from the places they go and this trash gets stuck in their roots. The trash represents the anger and hurt they feel. If this trash is not taken out of their roots, they will be unable to move and will be stuck. We are just like Tree People."

Continue with, "Sometimes we can get trash, in the form of anger, in our roots. To get the trash out of our roots, we must forgive others. If we are having difficulty forgiving others, we can say, 'God please help us forgive.' We can ask God to take away our anger. We can say,

'God please take away our anger.' We can tell those who hurt us, 'I forgive you. Please don't do that again.' Once we forgive others, our roots are clean and we are comfortable."

Show the family the *Tree People* page. Look at the Tree Person on the left hand side of the paper. Notice that the Tree Person is angry. Look at the *Tree People Resource* page. Look at the pictures and words on the *Tree People Resource* page and use them to help you identify those things that cause you to become angry. Color, cut, and glue the pictures that represent these situations in the boxes below the Tree Person's roots.

Look at the right hand side of the paper. This tree person looks comfortable. Look at the pictures and words on t*he Tree People Resource* page and use them to help you identify those things that help you change your feelings of anger to comfort. Color, cut out, and glue these pictures in the boxes in the thought bubbles.

Review the scripture verse with your family often.

Family Declaration: We declare that God's grace (unearned favor) is present in our lives. His grace is all we need. When others hurt us, we will forgive them just as God has forgiven us. When we take the high road God will vindicate any wrong done to us. The more we forgive, the more God's grace will bring healing and hope to our lives. God is restoring our relationships and rewarding our forgiveness. This is our declaration!

Champion: I declare that God's grace (unearned favor) is in my life. When I'm hurt, I will forgive just as God has forgiven me. The more I forgive, the more healing and hope are coming to my life. God is restoring my friendships and rewarding my forgiveness. This is my declaration!

Family Prayer – Read the family prayer together.

Dear God,

Thank You for loving us every day. Please help us to control our anger so we don't hurt anyone when we are angry. Please help us each day to clean out our roots by forgiving those who hurt us so we can feel comfortable again. Thank You for teaching us how to forgive. Amen.

The Unforgiving Servant
Scripture Card

Luke 11:4 - God forgives me, so I forgive everyone who has hurt me (adapted).

The Unforgiving Servant
Scripture Card

Once there was a king who found out one of his servants owed him a lot of money. The king found out that his servant didn't have enough money to pay his debt so the king decided to punish the servant.

When the servant came to see the king, the servant fell on the ground before the king and begged him to be patient with him. He promised that he would repay the king everything he owed him. The king felt compassion for the servant so he told the servant he didn't have to pay his debt.

That same day, the man the king forgave, saw someone who owed him a few dollars. He grabbed the man and said if he didn't pay him immediately, he would make sure he went to jail.

When the king found out what had happened, he was very angry. He had hoped that his servant would show the same mercy that he was shown. Because he did not, the king had the servant thrown in jail.

Jesus said that this is how the Heavenly Father will treat us if we refuse to forgive the people who hurt us. We have been forgiven. God expects us to forgive others. Adapted from Matthew 18:21-35.

Luke 11:4 - God forgives me, so I forgive everyone who has hurt me (adapted).

The Tree People

We are like the *Tree People*. Select pictures on the *Tree People Resource* page that have caused you to feel angry and hurt. Color, cut out, and glue these on the Tree Person's roots. You can clean out your roots by forgiving others who have hurt you and think of all the good things God has given you. Select pictures from the *Tree People Resource* page that help you to feel comfortable and glue them in the thought bubbles.

Tree People Resources

Anger   forgiveness

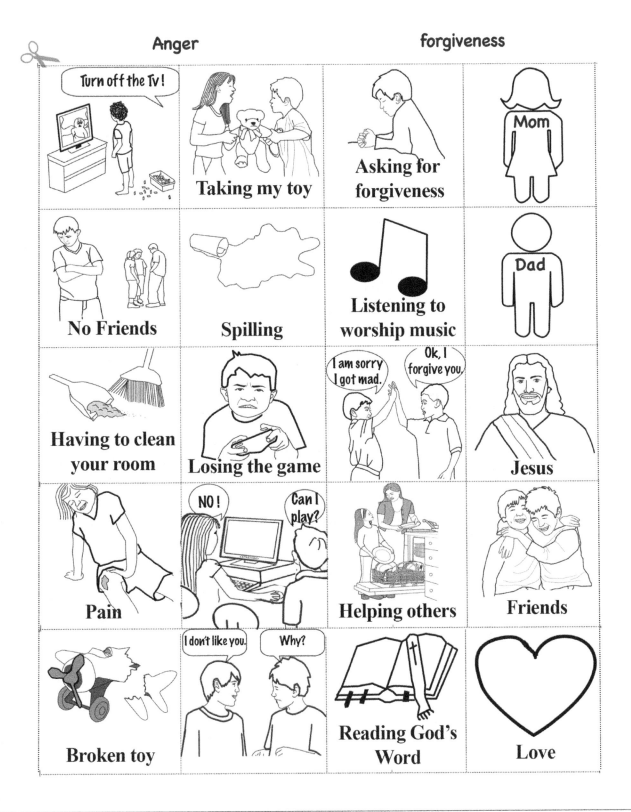

Devotional 28

Listening to God When I am Angry

Materials needed – white board and marker or a piece of paper, writing utensil, and anger and comfortable faces

Scripture - James 1:19 - *Everyone should be quick to listen, slow to speak, and slow to become angry (adapted).*

Goal - We will learn that when we are angry at someone or something, we need to listen to others before we say or do something.

Someone has hurt me. + I can be quick to listen, slow to speak, and slow to anger. = God is pleased.

Object lesson - Draw a human head on the white board with a dry erase marker or on a large sheet of paper. Include the eyes, nose, mouth, and ears in the drawing. Tell your family, "God made us with one mouth and two ears. We have twice as many ears as we have mouths. He wants us to be good listeners. Listening to others helps us control our anger. God wants us to be quick to listen, slow to speak, and slow to become angry."

Vocabulary development - Introduce the vocabulary words to the family. Talk about the meaning of each word. Acting out the meaning of the words through mime and gestures often increases the understanding of the concepts.

Listening - to pay attention to what someone is saying, making an effort to understand the meaning of the words spoken
Prophet - a person chosen by God to speak for God and guide His people
Anger - a strong feeling of being upset and frustration; an overwhelming feeling of fear or hurt

Bible Lesson - Look at the scripture card and point out the features of the picture while you read the Bible story out loud. Read the scripture out loud and have your family members repeat it several times. Color the scripture card together. Discuss the following with your family.

- Who was Jonah?
- What did God ask him to do? Why?
- What did he do instead?
- When Jonah disobeyed God what happened?
- When Jonah listened and obeyed God what happened to the people of Nineveh?

Application - Say, "It is important to listen to others when we are angry. Jonah should have listened to God instead of being angry at the people of Nineveh. When we listen to God and others it is easier to find an answer to a problem." Talk about a time when you were angry and you didn't listen to others. What happened? Could listening to others have helped you find a solution the problem? Choose a family member as your partner and role play an appropriate way to listen to others using the ***Listening to Others Conversation Cards***. Read each step out loud while acting it out. Remember to honor each other's personal space during the conversation.

Listening to Others Conversation Cards

Step 1: Face the person who is talking to you.

Step 2: Make eye contact with the person who is talking to you.

Step 3: Nod or smile when someone is talking to you.

Step 4: Ask a question about the topic.

Step 5: End the conversation.

Review the scripture verse with your family often.

Family Declaration: We declare we are going to listen to God, and not our feelings of anger. We will keep our joy in any situation. Instead of getting angry, we will look to God to give us the victory. When someone hurts us we will be slow to speak, and quick to listen. God will give us the right response in any circumstance. We are confident that we will overcome the challenge with God's guidance. We will move forward to our new level of destiny. This is our declaration!

Champion: I declare I will listen to God and not my feelings of anger. I will keep my joy no matter how hard it gets. When someone hurts me I will be slow to speak, and quick to listen to God. I know God is planning good things for my future. This is my declaration!

Family Prayer – Read the family prayer together.

Dear God,

Thank You for loving us no matter how we feel. You are a great God. Please help us listen to others. Thank You for listening to us. Amen.

Jonah Doesn't Listen to God
Scripture Card

James 1:19 - Everyone should be quick to listen, slow to speak, and slow to become angry (adapted).

Jonah Doesn't Listen to God
Scripture Card

Jonah was a prophet. God told Jonah to go to Nineveh and tell the people who lived in the city to stop doing bad things. He said that they should ask God to forgive them or He would destroy the city. Jonah didn't want to go because the people who lived in Nineveh had done bad things to the people related to Jonah and He was angry at the people.

Jonah didn't listen to God. He got on a boat that would take him far away from Nineveh. While Jonah was on the boat, God caused a great storm to come. The other people on the boat were afraid. Jonah told them that the storm came because he didn't listen to and obey God. Jonah went overboard into the sea. As soon as he was in the water, God caused a whale to swallow him. He was in the whale's belly for three days.

While Jonah was in the whale's belly, he told God he was sorry for not listening to Him or obeying Him. After the third day, the whale spat Jonah out onto the shore of Nineveh.

Jonah told the people in the city of Nineveh to stop doing bad things and ask God to forgive them. The people of Nineveh asked God to forgive them and they stopped doing bad things. God forgave them and He didn't destroy the city.
Adapted from Jonah chapters 1-3.

James 1:19 - Everyone should be quick to listen, slow to speak, and slow to become angry (adapted).

Listening To Others Conversation Cards

Use the *Listening to Others Conversation Cards* as you model how to listen to others.

1 When someone is talking to me, I stand facing him. My nose, knees, and toes face the nose, knees and toes of the person I am talking to.

LISTENING CARDS

2 When someone is talking to me, I look at his eyes. If I can't do this, I can look at the person's nose or forehead.

LISTENING CARDS

3 When someone is talking to me, I can nod or smile at him letting him know I am listening.

LISTENING CARDS

4 When someone is talking to me, I can ask questions about the topic of the conversation.

LISTENING CARDS

Devotional 29

Controlling My Anger

Materials needed – medium size ball that bounces, black permanent marker, and anger and comfortable faces

Scripture - Ephesians 4:26 - *In your anger do not sin.*

Goal - We will learn how to control our anger so we don't sin when we are angry.

I am angry. + I can control my anger with God's help. = God is pleased.

Object lesson - Write the word "Anger" in permanent marker on a medium sized ball. Begin bouncing the ball around the room slowly so you can control the ball. Say, "Being angry and controlling your anger is like bouncing a ball slowly. When you are angry and you control your anger, no one gets hurt."

Begin to bounce the ball with more force and let the ball get out of your grasp. Tell your family, "Having the ball bounce out of control is like when our anger is out of control. You and others around you could get hurt. Sometimes when we are angry and we don't control our anger, we make bad decisions. We may hurt others, destroy their property, and/or call them bad names. God wants us to remain in control of our anger."

Vocabulary development - Introduce the vocabulary words to the family. Talk about the meaning of each word. Acting out the meaning of the words through mime and gestures increases the understanding of the concepts.

Altar - a raised table in which sacrifices are offered to God
Temper - uncontrolled anger
Sacrifice - an act of offering something that we value to God
Anger - a strong feeling of being upset and frustration; an overwhelming feeling of fear or hurt

Bible Lesson - Look at the scripture card and point out the features of the picture while you read the Bible story out loud. Read the scripture out loud and have your family members repeat it several times. Color the scripture card together. Discuss the following with your family.

- Who were Cain and Abel?
- What did God ask Cain and Abel to do?
- Why did God accept Abel's sacrifice and not Cain's?
- What did Cain do to his brother? Why?
- What did God do to Cain because of his actions?

Application - Say, "There are many ways to control our anger. When we are angry, we can think about how much God loves us, how He accepts us, how He protects us, and how He always forgives us. Another tool we can use to help us control our anger is a fidget toy/object." Fidget toys/objects are available at local stores or online. Families can make their own fidget toys/objects.

Encourage your family members to make Take It Easy (TIE) balls by following the directions below. Use the TIE ball when needed as a tool to control your anger.

Materials needed for one ball: 3-5 small, round balloons, 2/3 cups of rice per balloon, 1 funnel

Step 1- Obtain 3-5 balloons.

Step 2- Blow the first balloon up slightly to stretch it out. Then, insert a funnel and fill the balloon with 2/3 cup of rice.

Step 3- Tie the end of the balloon into a tight knot. Snip off the excess balloon.

Step 4- Take another balloon of a different color. Cut off the neck of the balloon, and cut a few small holes into it. Pull the new balloon over the rice-filled one, covering the knot.

Step 5- Add another layer to the ball by repeating step four.

Step 6- Finally, test the ball by squeezing it. Add more layers if desired. (Oberkreser, L., 2013).

Review the scripture verse with your family often.

Family Declaration: We declare God is taking control of our emotions. Instead of getting angry with the circumstances in our lives, we will treat each day like it's a gift from God. His plans for us are for good and not evil. He wants us to live happy and content. When I give God control, He will turn what was meant for our harm into something good. Our hearts rejoice over the amazing plans God has for our future. This is our declaration!

Champion: I declare God is taking control of my emotions. Instead of getting angry with what is happening in my life, I will treat each day like it's a gift from God. His plans for me are for good and not evil. When I give God control of my anger, He will turn what was meant for my harm into something good. I am going to be better than I was before. This is my declaration!

Family Prayer – Read the family prayer together.

Dear God,

Thank You for giving us the ability to feel things and have emotions. Help us learn how to control our feelings of anger so we don't hurt others when we are angry at them. Thank You for always being close by when we need Your help. Amen.

Cain and his Uncontrolled Anger
Scripture Card

Ephesians 4:26 - In your anger do not sin.

Cain and his Uncontrolled Anger
Scripture Card

Adam and Eve were the first man and woman God created. They had two sons. The older son they named Cain and his brother was named Abel.

When Cain got older he became a farmer. He grew things from the ground. When Abel grew up he became a shepherd. He took care of the sheep. God blessed them so much they wanted to do something for God. They built an altar to make sacrifices to God.

A sacrifice is when you give something to God that you would have liked to keep for yourself. You give God your very best. Abel gave his best to God and Cain didn't. God accepted Abel's sacrifice, but He didn't accept Cain's sacrifice. Cain became very angry.

God loved Cain, and he said to him, "Why are you angry? Why do you look so sad and depressed?" If you had sacrificed your best, your sacrifice would have been accepted. You didn't sacrifice your best so it was not accepted. Cain didn't listen to God and he didn't control his anger.

Cain began to have bad thoughts. These thoughts resulted in him feeling very angry. His anger resulted in him making a very bad decision. He killed his brother, Abel.

Later that day God found Cain working in the hot sun. God asked him where his brother Abel was. Cain lied and said he didn't know. But God knew the terrible thing Cain had done. God saw Abel's blood on the ground.

God told Cain that because he spilled his brother's blood onto the ground, the ground wouldn't grow his crops anymore. From now on he would have to wander to faraway places to find his food. God also put a mark on Cain so everyone would know he was cursed and they wouldn't kill him.

It's ok to be angry, but it's not ok to hurt others when you are angry. (Adapted from Genesis 4: 1-13).

Ephesians 4:26 – In your anger do not sin.

Devotional 30

I Can Be a Peacemaker

Materials needed – stickers or individually wrapped candy, or inexpensive small toys, tray, and anger and comfortable faces

Scripture - Mark 5:9 - *Happy are the peacemakers, for they will be called children of God (adapted).*

Goal - We will learn how to be a peacemaker.

My friend and I are angry with each other. + I can be a peacemaker. = God is pleased.

Object lesson - Have some stickers or individually wrapped candy, or inexpensive small toys your family enjoys on a tray in front of them. Ask your family members one at a time to select as many objects as they would like. Continue with the process until all the objects are gone. Ensure that someone has more objects than the others. Say, "I am so sorry, but it looks like there are no more stickers (or other objects) left. It seems like some people got more than others. How do you feel knowing that someone took more stickers/objects than you? Some of us might be a little angry." Point to the anger face. Say, "God wants us to all get along. To do this we need to find a way to solve the problem so that everyone feels comfortable." Show the comfortable face. Continue with, "To do this we need to find a way to solve problems in life so everyone feels comfortable?" Talk about some solutions. Ensure that someone mentions sharing the objects so that everyone has the same number of objects.

Now, redistribute the objects so that each person has the same number of objects. After the objects have been redistributed, ask your family how they feel? They probably feel comfortable. Say, "Finding a solution to the problem is what peacemakers do. Peacemakers are people who help stop arguments. They bring peace to a situation where people are angry."

Vocabulary development - Introduce the vocabulary words to the family. Talk about the meaning of each word. Acting out the meaning of the words through mime and gestures increases the understanding of the concepts.

Peacemaker - someone who helps prevent or stop an argument, a peace seeker
Peace - a period of time when no arguing, fighting, or disagreements occur
Argument - a discussion in which people have different opinions about something and become angry
Anger - a strong feeling of being upset and frustration; an overwhelming feeling of fear or hurt

Bible Lesson - Look at the scripture card and point out the features of the picture while you read the Bible story out loud. Read the scripture out loud and have your family members repeat it several times. Color the scripture card together. Discuss the following with your family.

- What did God tell Abram to do?
- Who went to the new land with Abram?
- What were Lot and Abram's people arguing about?
- How did Abram act like a peacemaker?
- How did God reward Abram for his behavior?

Application - Say, "It's great when we are with our friends and family and everyone is getting along and having fun. We are happy and comfortable. Sometimes things happen and fights and arguments occur. Some things that could result in an argument are as follows.

- Someone wants something I have and takes it without asking to borrow it.
- Someone is saying mean things to us.
- Someone is saying mean things to our friends or family members.
- Someone is trying to hurt us.
- Someone doesn't take turns."

Encourage your family members to share about a time when they had an argument with someone. Tell your family, "There are several steps to follow when we want to be a peacemaker." Read and follow the steps on the *Peacemaker Conversation Cards* as you practice being a peacemaker with your family. Say, "Be a peacemaker this week with your family and friends. This pleases God."

Review the scripture verse with your family often.

Family Declaration: We declare we are God's peacemakers. God's peace is flowing out of us everyday to calm the storms we may face. We were created to make this world a better place. God will direct our steps and give us opportunities to be a blessing to others. A peace that will pass all understanding will help us meet needs and lift someone's spirit. We will keep our eyes open to be a calming presence and a light to those around us. This is our declaration!

Champion: I declare I am God's peacemaker. God's peace is flowing through me to help others. I was created to make this world a better place. I will look for ways to be a blessing to others each day. This is my declaration!

Family Prayer – Read the family prayer together.

Dear God,

Thank You for Jesus, our Prince of Peace. Please help us be like You and be peacemakers. Teach us how to find ways to solve problems and arguments. Thank You for the peace you give us each day. Amen.

Abram is a Peacemaker
Scripture Card

Mark 5:9 – Happy are the peacemakers, for they will be called children of God (adapted).

Abram is a Peacemaker
Scripture Card

God told Abram to leave his home and go to a new land. Abram, his wife Sarah, and his nephew Lot packed up everything they owned and began to walk to their new home. Abram had many sheep, cattle, camels, and goats, and so did Lot. There were so many sheep, Abram and Lot had their own shepherds.

After a long journey, Abram and Lot with all their animals, shepherds, and servants arrived at their new home. Everything was great until Lot and Abram's shepherds started arguing. There wasn't enough food for all the animals to eat because they were all together in a small area. Abram wanted to stop the fighting and be a peacemaker, so he came up with a way to fix the problem. He saw that there was a lot of land off in the distance. He told Lot to choose the land he wanted and Abram would take the land that was left over.

Lot took the best land and moved there with all of his animals, shepherds, and servants. Abram stayed where he was. After Lot left, God told Abram that all the land he could see would be his forever. God promised that Abram would have many descendants. Abram was very happy. Adapted from Genesis 13: 1-16.

Mark 5:9 – Happy are the peacemakers, for they will be called children of God (adapted).

Peacemaker Conversation Cards

Use the *Peacemaker Conversation Cards* as you model the steps to follow to bring peace to any situation.

1 Ask God to help you. You can say, "God, please help me be a peacemaker. Take away my anger now."

2 What is the problem? What are we fighting about?

3 Talk about ways to fix the problem.

Try one.

4 If the problem is fixed, praise God for peace. If it isn't fixed, try another way to solve the problem.

Devotional 31

Get the Facts Before You Get Angry

Materials needed – black marker and anger and comfortable faces

Scripture - Proverbs 29:11 - *A fool always loses his temper, but a wise man holds it back.*

Goal - We will learn that it is wise to ask questions about a situation before we get angry.

I am angry. + I can get all the facts before I act. = I can be comfortable again.

Object lesson - Before you begin the object lesson, write a large question mark on the palms of both your hands. Make sure to let the ink dry before you begin the lesson. Don't let your family members see the question marks. Say, "When we are angry, it feels like this." Have your family members clap their hands together and begin rubbing them back and forth slowly at first then more quickly. Continue with, "You will notice that as you rub your hands together they begin to get warm just like we feel when we are angry. Before our hands get too hot it is a good idea to stop rubbing them together and ask questions." Show your family the palms of your hands. Make sure they see the question marks and understand what the question mark means. Continue with, "When we ask questions to get more information, we can get answers about how and why things happen and that can help us control our anger. When you are angry, it is a good idea to ask questions about the situation before you say or do something that may hurt someone else. "

Vocabulary development - Introduce the vocabulary words to the family. Talk about the meaning of each word. Acting out the meaning of the words through mime and gestures increases the understanding of the concepts.

Persecute - to treat others badly by calling them names or hitting them
Apostle - any important early leader of the faith
Anger - a strong feeling of being upset and frustration; an overwhelming feeling of fear or hurt

Bible Lesson - Look at the scripture card and point out the features of the picture while you read the Bible story out loud. Read the scripture out loud and have your family members repeat it several times. Color the scripture card together. Discuss the following with your family.

- What was Saul doing to the Christians? Why?
- What happened on the road to Damascus?
- Who is Ananias? What did he do for Saul?
- What did Paul do when he became a Christian?

Application- Have some family members share about a time when they were angry and hurt others. Talk about how asking questions may have stopped them from hurting others. Make sure to emphasize how important it is to ask questions to get more information about a situation before we let our anger get out of control and hurt others. Participate in the following role play activity with your family.

Before the role play, identify each character and the setting. After the role play is complete, reinforce the key concept of the devotional.

When I am Angry, I Can Ask Questions

Characters: Narrator, Roxy, Joe (Roxy's brother,) Ali (Roxy's sister) -The names may be changed to the names of the people actually participating in this activity.

Setting: At home

Narrator: Roxy, Joe, and Ali are at home relaxing. Roxy walks to the refrigerator to get the ice cream she saved for dessert. Ali is sitting at the kitchen table.

Roxy: (opens the freezer and yells) Who ate my ice cream?

Joe: (walks into the kitchen) I didn't touch it.

Ali: I didn't eat your ice cream.

Roxy: (yells loudly) Ali, I know you ate my ice cream. You are a liar!

Ali: I didn't eat your ice cream and I don't like it when you yell at me. It hurts my feelings.

Roxy: I am yelling at you because you make me so angry. I was saving that ice cream for dessert. Now what am I going to eat for dessert?

Joe: (looking in the freezer) Hey, look I found your ice cream. It was behind the frozen peas. Mom went shopping yesterday so she must have moved the ice cream to make room for more food.

Roxy: I am so sorry for yelling at you guys. I am sorry for calling you a liar Ali.

Narrator: Roxy learned a lesson today. She learned that before she gets angry and begins to make bad choices like calling someone a name, she needs to ask questions. She could have asked if anyone had seen her ice cream instead of accusing others of eating it.

Read the scripture with your family often.

Family Declaration: We declare God is with us and will show us the truth. Even in times of hurt or disappointment, we are not alone. He will never leave us wondering, confused, or discouraged. As we are honest with Him about our doubts and fears, He will provide a way out of every situation. God is helping us with the things we don't understand. He will give us the facts and help us make the right choices. He will restore our faith and guide our hearts. This is our declaration!

Champion: I declare God is with me and will show me the truth. When I am feeling hurt, disappointed, or angry I am not alone. When I talk to God about my feelings, He will provide a way out of every situation. God will give me the facts so I can make the right choices. He will restore my faith and guide my heart. This is my declaration!

Family Prayer- Read the family prayer together.

Dear God,

Thank You for giving us feelings. Please help us to express our feelings without hurting others. Help us learn to how to ask questions when we are angry so we can make good choices. Thank You for loving us no matter how we are feeling. Amen.

Saul Learns the Facts
Scripture Card

Proverbs 15:1 - A fool always loses his temper, but a wise man holds it back.

Saul Learns the Facts
Scripture Card

Many years ago, there was a man whose name was Saul. He thought that Jesus and His followers were evil. He didn't listen to anyone who tried to tell him that he was wrong. He was an enemy of the people who believed that Jesus was the Son of God. He did many terrible things to the followers of Jesus.

One day as Saul was traveling to the city of Damascus to find and hurt Christians, a bright light appeared and he fell to the ground. He heard the voice of Jesus saying, "Saul why are you persecuting me?" Saul answered, "Who are you Lord?" Jesus replied, "I am Jesus whom you are persecuting. Now get up and go into the city, and you will be told what you must do." Saul got up from the ground, but when he opened his eyes he couldn't see anything. So the men he was traveling with lead him into Damascus.

In Damascus there was a Christian named Ananias. God told him that Saul was coming to his city and he should help him. Ananias was afraid to do this because he had heard about what Saul did to Christians. Jesus told him He was going to use Saul to tell many people about Jesus.

Ananias went to where Saul was staying and prayed for him. Immediately Saul was able to see again. Saul accepted Jesus as his personal Savior and was baptized in water. Saul regained his strength. His life was changed forever. He realized that he should have asked questions and listened to others before getting angry. His anger towards those who followed Jesus changed. He felt very sorry for hurting all the people he did.

When Saul became a Christian, he began to use his other name which was Paul so everyone would know he was a new man. Paul went from city to city telling everyone about how Jesus loves them and died for their sins. Paul began several churches and wrote 14 books in the New Testament. He became one of the most well-known apostles.

Proverbs 15:1 – A fool always loses his temper, but a wise man holds it back.

When I am Angry, I Can Ask Questions Script

Characters: Narrator, Roxy, Joe (Roxy's brother,) Ali (Roxy's sister) -The names may be changed to the names of the people actually participating in this activity.

Setting: At home

Narrator: Roxy, Joe, and Ali are at home relaxing. Roxy walks to the refrigerator to get the ice cream she saved for dessert. Ali is sitting at the kitchen table.

Roxy: (opens the freezer and yells) Who ate my ice cream?

Joe: (walks into the kitchen) I didn't touch it.

Ali: I didn't eat your ice cream.

Roxy: (yells loudly) Ali, I know you ate my ice cream. You are a liar!

Ali: I didn't eat your ice cream and I don't like it when you yell at me. It hurts my feelings.

Roxy: I am yelling at you because you make me so angry. I was saving that ice cream for dessert. Now what am I going to eat for dessert?

Joe: (looking in the freezer) Hey, look I found your ice cream. It was behind the frozen peas. Mom went shopping yesterday so she must have moved the ice cream to make room for more food.

Roxy: I am so sorry for yelling at you guys. I am sorry for calling you a liar Ali.

Narrator: Roxy learned a lesson today. She learned that before she gets angry and begins to make bad choices like calling someone a name, she needs to ask questions. She could have asked if anyone had seen her ice cream instead of accusing others of eating it.

References

Creative Youth Ideas. (2014). Object Lesson-Jelly Bean Salvation. Retrieved from
http://www.slideshare.net/kensapp/object-lesson-jelly-bean-salvation.

Guenther, Leanee. (2013). Jesus is Alive. Retrieved from
http://www.dltk- bible.com/cv/jesus_is_alive_cv.htm.

Lindsay Hawkes. (2013). Object Lessons that help explain Easter to kids. Retrieved from
http://www.focusonthefamily.ca/parenting/school-age/three-fun-object-lessons-
that-help-explain-easter-to-kids.

Resources

Bible Stories for Kids

http://www.essex1.com/people/paul/bible.html

Stories to listen, watch, or read.

http://www.veggietales.com/

Kid Explorers

http://www.christiananswers.net/kids/menu-act.html
Games, Videos, Bible Stories, Coloring Pages, and kids movie reviews.

Veggies tales.com

About Funbrain http://www.funbrain.com/aboutus.html

Since 1997, kids, teachers, librarians, and parents have enthusiastically turned to Funbrain for its free educational games, online books, and comics. Funbrain, created for kids ages pre-school through grade 8, offers more than 100 fun, interactive games that develop skills in math, reading, and literacy. Plus, kids can read a variety of popular books and comics on the site, including Diary of a Wimpy Kid, Amelia Writes Again, and Brewster Rocket. 2000 -2014 Pearson Education, Inc. All rights reserved

We are all special to God.

www.wycliffekids

Wycliffe Kids is a website from Wycliffe Bible Translators created for kids. This site has many great activities for kids like games, puzzles, stories, and quizzes; you can go on adventures and find out about the Bible, John Wycliffe, and how missionaries translate the Bible today. Children and young adults can learn how to help missionaries today.

Made in the USA
Columbia, SC
26 May 2019